Rivers Reunited

Rivers Reunited

Kaleshwaram's Triumph

Rafeal Mechlore

UNIEK ENTERPRISES

CONTENTS

INDEX

1. Execution of the massive project
2. Overcoming hurdles and setbacks

Chapter 4 Impact on Agriculture

1. Agricultural Transformation
1. Improved irrigation and crop patterns
2. Increased agricultural productivity

B. Socio-economic Upliftment

1. Changes in livelihoods and rural communities
2. Alleviating poverty through water access

Chapter 5 Environmental Considerations

1. Ecological Impact
1. Effects on local ecosystems and biodiversity
2. Measures taken to minimize harm

B. Sustainability Measures

1. Long-term sustainability and water management
2. Balancing development and ecology

Chapter 6 Challenges and Controversies

1. Political and Environmental Opposition
1. Critics and concerns
2. The project's response to controversies

B. Technical Challenges

1. Lessons learned and innovations
2. Future-proofing the Kaleshwaram Project

Chapter 7 Success Stories

1. Personal Narratives

1. Stories from beneficiaries
2. Changed lives and futures

B. Economic Growth

1. Economic development in the region
2. Infrastructure and industry growth

Chapter 8 Lessons for the World

1. Global Relevance
1. How Kaleshwaram's success can inspire other regions
2. Lessons for sustainable water management

B. Future Prospects

1. The role of Kaleshwaram in India's water future
2. Evolving challenges and opportunities

INTRODUCTION

Water, the quintessence of life, has held a hallowed spot in mankind's set of experiences and progress since days of yore. Its stream, or deficiency in that department, has formed societies, affected relocations, and decided the predetermination of countries. No place is this more apparent than in the Indian subcontinent, where waterways have not exclusively been wellsprings of food yet in addition objects of love and legend. India's streams are essential to its character, culture, and economy. They have supported the land and its kin for centuries, supporting the agrarian heartland and encouraging assorted biological systems.

Be that as it may, the narrative of India's streams is certainly not a direct one. A mind boggling story wavers among overflow and shortage, immersion and dry spell. The subcontinent's huge organization of waterways, while a wellspring of overflow during the storm season, can rapidly transform into a wellspring of decimation when the downpours neglect to show up. This tricky equilibrium has made water the executives a ceaseless test for Indian legislatures, requiring visionary ventures to saddle, circulate, and defend this valuable asset.

In the chronicles of India's water history, there stands an exceptional demonstration of **human creativity and assurance:** the Kaleshwaram Task. This stupendous endeavor, arranged in the core of the Indian province of Telangana, has arisen as an encouraging sign and an image of win in the domain of water asset the board. The Kaleshwaram Venture addresses the nervy quest for subduing streams as well as joining them — an accomplishment that can possibly reshape the predetermination of a locale long tormented by water shortage and farming vulnerability.

The reason for this book is to dig profound into the account of Kaleshwaram, investigating its beginning, its designing wonders, the significant effect it has had on horticulture and society, the difficulties it has confronted, and the debates it has lighted. Through careful exploration, individual stories, master interviews, and an all encompassing perspective on the undertaking's verifiable and contemporary setting, we expect to introduce a complete record of Kaleshwaram's victory — a victory that represents the overcoming of streams as well as the vanquishing of misfortune and the acknowledgment of a visionary dream.

Laying everything out

To comprehend the meaning of the Kaleshwaram Venture, it is basic to lay the right foundation by examining the significant significance of streams in India's social,

authentic, and ecological embroidery. The Indian subcontinent is supplied with a huge number of streams, each with its own special person and importance. From the powerful Ganges, thought about the holiest stream by Hindus, to the nurturing Yamuna, the sacrosanct Saraswati, and the worshipped Godavari, these water bodies have molded India's otherworldly and social ethos.

The Meaning of Streams in India

Streams are not simply collections of streaming water in India; they are venerated goddesses, divine life savers that have tracked down notice in antiquated sacred writings and stories. The Rigveda, perhaps of the most seasoned text on the planet, praises the may and blessedness of the Sindhu (Indus) Waterway. The Mahabharata, another old epic, portrays the excursion of the Pandavas along the banks of the Ganges. These stories underline the otherworldly association that waterways hold in the Indian mind.

Past otherworldliness, waterways are crucial for agribusiness, which is the foundation of India's economy. The rich alluvial fields watered by these waterways have supported developments for centuries, supporting a blossoming populace. The yearly storm downpours, took care of by the Indian Sea, fill these streams, transforming parched scenes into flourishing rural heartlands.

Nonetheless, this occasional overflow is joined by the enduring danger of floods, frequently prompting devastating death toll and property. Subsequently, the conundrum of bounty and danger is a common subject in India's relationship with its waterways.

The Verifiable Setting of Water The board

Over India's time, rulers, and pioneers have wrestled with the difficulties of water the executives. The old Mauryan Realm, under the visionary Head Chandragupta Maurya, is accepted to have built one of the earliest water system frameworks in India. The stepwells of the Indus Valley Progress stand as quiet declaration to the old designing ability in water the executives.

Quick forward to the archaic time, and we experience the grand reservoir conduits and stepwells of the Mughal Domain, which exhibited the combination of feel and usefulness in water engineering. These designing wonders extinguished the thirst of urban areas as well as given break to exhausted explorers.

The English provincial time frame saw the foundation of the primary methodical ways to deal with water asset the board. Waterways and dams were developed, frequently to the detriment of neighborhood networks and biological systems. The pioneer tradition of water administration in India established the groundwork for present day water foundation improvement, which keeps on developing today.

In contemporary times, India faces a remarkable arrangement of difficulties with respect to its streams. Quick urbanization, industrialization, and populace development have put colossal strain on water assets. Environmental change has made the storm designs progressively flighty, prompting more successive and serious dry seasons and floods. Water contamination, generally coming from unrestrained industrialization and deficient waste administration, represents a danger to both human wellbeing and biological system honesty.

Against this background of verifiable veneration, rural reliance, and contemporary difficulties, the Kaleshwaram Venture arises as a turning point — a victory that tries to address a portion of India's most squeezing water-related issues. This book expects to disentangle the unpredictable embroidery of this striking task, revealing insight into the visionaries behind it, the designing wonders that make it conceivable, the extraordinary effect it has had, and the illustrations it offers for maintainable water the executives in India as well as across the world.

Allow us to set out on an excursion through the heartlands of Telangana, where waterways were not recently subdued; they were brought together, carrying trust and flourishing to a dry land. Welcome to the narrative of Streams Rejoined: Kaleshwaram's Victory.

Chapter 1

Setting the Scene

In the immense embroidery of mankind's set of experiences, hardly any components have assumed as significant a part as water. From the beginning of human progress to the cutting edge time, water has been the wellspring of life as well as an impetus for the ascent and fall of social orders. As we set out on an excursion to investigate the narrative of the Kaleshwaram Task, it is vital to lay everything out by digging profound into the immortal meaning of water in human life and the verifiable setting of water the executives.

Water: The Pith of Life

Water, the all inclusive dissolvable, is the support of life on The planet. It is the actual pith of presence, a valuable asset that supports the natural variety of our planet as well as the social and social variety of human social orders. The human body itself is made out of around 60% water, underlining the private association among water and life.

Over the entire course of time, water has been both a wellspring of sustenance and a power of change. Old developments, from the Mesopotamians to the Egyptians and the Indus Valley individuals, thrived along the banks of streams, where the fruitful soil and bountiful water assets worked with farming and settlement.

Water has likewise been a wellspring of motivation and profound importance across societies. In India, the consecrated waterways of the Ganges, Yamuna, Saraswati, and Godavari are respected as goddesses, exemplifying virtue, eternality, and the pattern of life and passing. Explorers rush to these waterways to purge their transgressions, perform ceremonies, and look for profound illumination.

Past its social and profound significance, water is a monetary force to be reckoned with. Horticulture, the foundation of numerous economies, relies upon a predictable and dependable inventory of water. Streams, with their occasional streams and nurturing properties, have been the essential wellspring of water system for quite a long time. They have powered the development of civic establishments and the success of countries.

In any case, the connection among people and water isn't one of unrestrained amicability. The very waterways that bring life and flourishing during the storm season can unleash devastation when they flood their banks. Floods, a common cataclysmic event, have molded the course of history by obliterating urban communities, uprooting populaces, and changing scenes.

Basically, water is a situation with two sides — a provider of life and a harbinger of obliteration. The test over the entire course of time has been to bridle the life-supporting parts of water while relieving the disastrous ones. This challenge has led to the science and specialty of water the executives.

Water The board Through the Ages

The historical backdrop of water the executives is a demonstration of human inventiveness, diligence, and versatility. As social orders developed and turned out to be more complicated, so did their requirement for coordinated water frameworks. Water the board developed from straightforward wells and reservoir conduits to refined water system organizations and super dams.

Antiquated Water The board

In old times, water the executives was basically confined and limited scope. Individuals assembled wells to get to groundwater, made patios to control soil disintegration, and created simple water system frameworks to redirect water from waterways and streams to their fields. The Indus Valley Civilization, one of the world's earliest metropolitan developments, is known for its high level water the executives strategies, incorporating very much arranged urban communities with coordinated waste frameworks.

Roman Water systems and Showers

The Romans raised water designing higher than ever with their reservoir conduits, which moved new water over significant distances to metropolitan focuses. The Roman showers, a necessary piece of their way of life, were mind boggling frameworks that expected a steady inventory of water. These advancements worked on general wellbeing as well as added to the development of Roman urban areas.

Archaic Waterworks

In bygone eras, especially in bone-dry locales, social orders went to shrewd strategies to augment water use. One of the most momentous models is the qanat framework, created in Persia (cutting edge Iran). Qanats were underground passages that took advantage of groundwater sources, giving a dependable stockpile of water for horticulture and metropolitan settlements.

The English Frontier Heritage

The English frontier time frame made a permanent imprint on India's water the executives frameworks. The English, perceiving the significance of water for farming efficiency and transportation, fabricated broad channel organizations and dams across the subcontinent. These tasks, while adding to financial turn of events, additionally upset nearby environments and networks.

Present day Water Framework

In the cutting edge period, water the board has turned into a multi-disciplinary field that consolidates designing, hydrology, natural science, and strategy. Dams, supplies, and water system projects have become gigantic endeavors, frequently including worldwide collaboration and huge ventures of capital and HR.

Water the executives isn't restricted to giving water to horticulture and metropolitan use; it likewise incorporates flood control, water cleaning, wastewater treatment, and protection endeavors. Moreover, the difficulties of environmental change, populace development, and urbanization have added new layers of intricacy to the field.

In India, the tradition of water the board is profoundly weaved with its way of life and history. The subcontinent's immense waterway frameworks, including the Ganges, Yamuna, Brahmaputra, and Godavari, have been the backbone of the land for centuries. They have fed the fields, empowered exchange and transportation, and upheld assorted biological systems.

However, India's relationship with its waterways has been set apart by both worship and battle. The storm downpours, while fundamental for farming, are famously erratic. The overflow of water during the blustery season is many times followed by intense water shortage during dry months. The test of dealing with this occasional fluctuation has driven the improvement of water foundation and approaches in India.

The Indian Stream Scene

The Ganges (Ganga): The Ganges is maybe the most respected waterway in India, considered the holiest of all. Its waters are accepted to scrub one's wrongdoings, and a life saver for a huge number of individuals live along its banks.

The Yamuna: The Yamuna, a significant feeder of the Ganges, is likewise thought to be consecrated and has a rich verifiable and social importance. It is related with Master Krishna and the city of Mathura.

The Saraswati: The Saraswati Waterway, however to a great extent legendary today, holds a unique spot in Hindu custom as the stream of information and shrewdness.

The Godavari: The Godavari is frequently alluded to as "Dakshin Ganga" or the Ganges of the South. It moves through a few states and supports farming, industry, and culture along its course.

These streams, among others, have molded the social, social, and monetary texture of India. They have given food to millions, worked with exchange and transportation, and motivated innumerable tunes, sonnets, and stories.

The Dubious Equilibrium of Water

India's reliance on its waterways for food and success has forever been a fragile dance among overflow and shortage, flood and dry season. The storm season, which brings nurturing downpours, can likewise bring horrendous floods. Conversely, the dry season frequently prompts intense water deficiencies.

This dubious equilibrium has been both a gift and a revile. The yearly rainstorm are enthusiastically anticipated by ranchers, as they give the important water to planting and development. Nonetheless, a postponed or powerless rainstorm can bring about crop disappointments, food deficiencies, and financial pain.

Then again, over the top precipitation during the rainstorm can prompt annihilating floods, causing death toll and property. Streams break their banks, immersing towns and urban areas. Floods have been a common cataclysmic event in India, and the test of overseeing them has been a consistent subject in water the board.

Dry spell is another lasting test. At the point when the storm fizzles or is insufficient, water sources evaporate, and farming efficiency falls. Dry seasons have a flowing impact, prompting food shortage, monetary misery, and movement from country to metropolitan regions.

Fundamentally, India's waterways are both a wellspring of life and a wellspring of weakness. The pattern of overflow and shortage has driven social orders to foster inventive water the board procedures, from antiquated water collecting strategies to current dam development.

The Requirement for Visionary Undertakings

As India proceeds to develop and urbanize, the interest for water has flooded. Quick industrialization and metropolitan development have put massive strain on water assets. Environmental change, set apart by progressively unusual rainstorm designs, has made water the board considerably seriously testing.

In this unique situation, visionary water projects have become critical for India's reasonable turn of events. These tasks point not exclusively to address the quick

necessities of water supply, farming, and flood control yet additionally to guarantee long haul water security. They address the aggregate exertion of architects, researchers, policymakers, and networks to outfit the capability of waterways while relieving the dangers they present.

One such visionary undertaking, which remains as a demonstration of human desire and assurance, is the Kaleshwaram Task. Arranged in the core of the Indian territory of Telangana, the Kaleshwaram Venture addresses the brassy quest for restraining streams as well as joining them — an accomplishment that can possibly reshape the predetermination of a locale long tormented by water shortage and horticultural vulnerability.

The Kaleshwaram Venture is something beyond a foundation try; it is an image of trust, a harbinger of flourishing, and a victory of human resourcefulness over nature's eccentricity. A story should be told — an account of visionaries who hoped against hope, engineers who pushed the limits of plausibility, and a locale that has been everlastingly changed by the reunification of its waterways.

As we leave on this excursion to disentangle the narrative of Streams Rejoined: Kaleshwaram's Victory, we will dive profound into the beginning of the undertaking, the designing wonders that make it conceivable, the groundbreaking effect it has had on horticulture and society, the difficulties it has confronted, and the contentions it has lighted. Through fastidious exploration, individual stories, master interviews, and an all encompassing perspective on the venture's verifiable and contemporary setting, we expect to introduce an exhaustive record of Kaleshwaram's victory — a victory that represents the vanquishing of waterways as well as the overcoming of difficulty and the acknowledgment of a visionary dream.

Welcome to the heartlands of Telangana, where streams were not recently restrained; they were brought together, carrying trust and flourishing to a dry land. Welcome to the account of Waterways Rejoined: Kaleshwaram's Victory.

1. **The significance of rivers in India**

    Streams hold a significant importance in the social, environmental, and monetary texture of India. Frequently alluded to as the "support of civilization," India's stream frameworks play had a vital impact in molding the country's set of experiences, culture, and lifestyle for millennia. These grand water bodies are a wellspring of life as well as a wellspring of motivation, otherworldliness, and food for individuals of India.

    Environmental Importance:

    Biodiversity: India's waterways are abounding with different types of life, both widely varied vegetation. They give a crucial territory to innumerable types of plants and creatures. The riverbanks and floodplains are wealthy in biodiversity, supporting various types of fish, birds, and oceanic plants.

    Water supply: The streams in India are an essential wellspring of freshwater. They supply water for drinking, water system, and modern use. Horticulture, the foundation of the Indian economy, vigorously depends on stream water for crop development. Besides, the accessibility of freshwater is fundamental for human endurance and advancement.

    Disintegration control: Streams assume an essential part in controlling soil disintegration. The progression of water helps in diverting dregs and forestalling the debasement of rich land. This viewpoint is especially imperative in a country with broad farming area.

    Social Importance:

    Otherworldly significance: Waterways are viewed as consecrated in Indian culture. The Ganges, Yamuna, Saraswati, and numerous different streams are adored as goddesses, and a huge number of individuals participate in customs and services along their banks. Washing in these heavenly streams is accepted to purge one's transgressions and lead to profound refinement.

Verifiable significance: Large numbers of India's old civilizations prospered along the banks of streams. The Indus Valley Civilization, one of the world's most seasoned, created along the Indus Waterway. The Ganges and Yamuna have been key to the development of civilizations in northern India. These waterways have seen the ascent and fall of domains, the introduction of religions, and the advancement of workmanship and culture.

Social variety: Waterways have been instrumental in forming the different societies and customs of India. Various locales along the course of a waterway have their own novel traditions, celebrations, and cooking styles, adding to India's rich social embroidery.

Financial Importance:

Agribusiness: India's horticulture area vigorously depends on stream water for water system. The fruitful alluvial soil kept by streams like the Ganges, Brahmaputra, and

Godavari has made these locales the breadbasket of India. Significant yields like rice, wheat, sugarcane, and cotton are filled bounteously here.

Transportation: By and large, waterways filled in as crucial shipping lanes. Indeed, even today, they are fundamental for transportation, working with the development of products and individuals. Significant urban communities like Kolkata, Varanasi, and Mumbai owe their essential areas and monetary importance to the streams coursing through them.

Hydroelectric power: A few waterways in India are tackled for hydroelectric power age. Dams and repositories based on streams like the Bhagirathi and Sutlej produce power, adding to the country's energy needs.

Difficulties and Dangers:

Contamination: Numerous waterways in India experience the ill effects of extreme contamination because of modern release, untreated sewage, and rural overflow. This contamination hurts the environment as well as stances serious wellbeing dangers to the populace depending on these streams for drinking water.

Dams and redirections: The development of dams and redirections for water system and power age has changed the normal progression of numerous streams. This disturbs the waterway environments and can have downstream outcomes.

Environmental change: Changing weather conditions, including sporadic rainstorm and icy dissolve, influence the progression of waterways. This has suggestions for water accessibility and agribusiness.

Deforestation: The obliteration of backwoods in stream catchment regions adds to soil disintegration and sedimentation in waterways, influencing water quality and stream biological systems.

Over-extraction: Extreme extraction of groundwater for farming and modern use can prompt diminished stream in streams, worsening water shortage issues.

2. **The historical context of water management**

Water has been a basic asset for human social orders from the beginning of time, molding the course of developments, economies, and societies. The verifiable setting of water the board is an entrancing excursion that highlights the significance of water in

human turn of events and the development of social orders. From antiquated stream valley human advancements to present day modern countries, water the executives has been vital to endurance and progress.

Antiquated Waterway Valley Developments:

The starting points of water the board can be followed back to the world's most memorable extraordinary developments, which arose along the banks of streams. Mesopotamia, arranged between the Tigris and Euphrates streams, and the Indus Valley Human progress along the Indus Waterway, are among the earliest models.

Mesopotamia: The Sumerians, who occupied Mesopotamia around 4500 BCE, fostered a perplexing arrangement of trenches and dams to control the flighty flooding of the Tigris and Euphrates. These endeavors considered the development of yields, prompting overflow food creation, populace development, and the rise of urban communities.

Indus Valley Civilization: The Indus Valley Development, prospering around 3300-1300 BCE, highlighted progressed metropolitan preparation and modern water the board frameworks. The urban areas of Harappa and Mohenjo-Daro flaunted all around arranged roads, seepage frameworks, and repositories that gathered and conveyed water for different purposes, featuring the significance of water the executives in metropolitan turn of events.

Antiquated Egypt:

The Nile Stream assumed a critical part in the ascent of old Egypt. The yearly immersion of the Nile carried prolific sediment to the fields, permitting Egyptians to rehearse agribusiness. The development of channels, barriers, and supplies controlled the water stream, guaranteeing solid water system and empowering the development of a strong progress along the Nile's banks.

Roman Water channels:

The Roman Domain is prestigious for its amazing water passage frameworks. Romans designed immense organizations of reservoir conduits, channels, and passages to move water from far off sources to their urban areas. These reservoir conduits gave clean water to public showers, wellsprings, and confidential homes, exhibiting the significance of water the board for metropolitan life.

Archaic Islamic Commitments:

During the archaic period, Islamic researchers and architects made critical commitments to water the executives. Al-Jazari, a Middle Easterner designer in the twelfth 100 years, archived different water advances, including water-controlled gadgets for plants and siphons.

These developments further developed water dissemination and horticultural efficiency in locales under Islamic impact.

Archaic Europe:

In archaic Europe, primitive masters built elaborate water frameworks to drive plants, empowering the crushing of grain, cutting of lumber, and creation of different merchandise. Waterwheels, driven by streaming water, were utilized widely to tackle mechanical energy for different modern cycles.

Provincial America and Pressure driven Designing:

In provincial America, pressure driven designing assumed a urgent part in the improvement of settlements. Waterwheels and dams were utilized to control gristmills, sawmills, and material factories. These improvements denoted the starting points of industrialization in North America.

The Modern Transformation:

The eighteenth and nineteenth hundreds of years achieved the Modern Transformation, which significantly changed water the executives. Steam motors, at first fueled by coal, later progressed to involving water as an energy source. The development of broad waterway frameworks and supplies worked with the transportation of unrefined components and completed merchandise, driving monetary development.

Current Water The executives:

Dams and Repositories: Huge dams and supplies have been built overall to store water for water system, flood control, and hydropower age.

Desalination: In bone-dry districts, desalination advances have been formed to change over seawater into freshwater, tending to water shortage issues.

Wastewater Treatment: High level wastewater treatment plants have been laid out to treat and reuse sewage, diminishing natural contamination.

Water Protection: Attention to water preservation has developed, prompting endeavors to decrease water wastage in farming, industry, and families.

Environmental Change Variation: Environmental change has expanded the unconventionality of atmospheric conditions, requiring versatile water the executives techniques to alleviate dry seasons, floods, and other water-related difficulties.

B. Kaleshwaram Project: A Game-Changer

The Kaleshwaram Lift Water system Venture, situated in the Indian province of Telangana, remains as a surprising illustration of current designing and water asset the board. This enormous endeavor can possibly be a unique advantage for Telangana as well as for the whole district, resolving basic issues connected with water shortage, rural efficiency, and generally financial turn of events.

Project Outline:

The Kaleshwaram Task is one of the world's biggest multi-reason lift water system plans, intended to tackle the Godavari Stream's water and redirect it to bone-dry locales in Telangana. It was introduced in June 2019 and is named after the town of Kaleshwaram, where the central god, Master Shiva, is loved. The task includes an organization of channels, siphon houses, supplies, and pipelines, with a complete assessed cost of over Rs. 80,000 crore (around 11 billion USD).

Key Highlights:

Siphon Houses: The venture brags an organization 20 siphon houses, each outfitted with various high-limit siphons. These siphons lift water from the Godavari Stream to the capacity repositories and trenches, guaranteeing water accessibility consistently.

Repositories: Numerous capacity supplies and tanks have been developed to store and circulate the redirected water. These repositories assist with controlling the progression of water, guaranteeing a consistent stockpile for water system and drinking water purposes.

Trenches and Pipelines: The task incorporates a broad organization of channels and pipelines that circulate water to the farthest corners of the state. These channels range huge number of kilometers, giving water to both agrarian and metropolitan regions.

Game-Evolving Effect:

Horticulture: Telangana has generally been a district inclined to water shortage, restricting rural efficiency. The Kaleshwaram Venture will give a steady and dependable water supply for water system, helping a great many ranchers. Expanded agrarian result is supposed to further develop food security and lift country salaries.

Monetary Turn of events: Further developed water system and water supply will animate financial development. With the expanded accessibility of water, ventures, for example, materials, food handling, and assembling are supposed to prosper, making position and adding to the state's economy.

Drinking Water Supply: The task will likewise address drinking water deficiencies in both provincial and metropolitan regions. Spotless and open drinking water is fundamental for general wellbeing and prosperity, and the undertaking intends to give this essential need to a huge piece of the populace.

Dry season Relief: Telangana has encountered extreme dry spells previously, prompting crop disappointments and trouble among ranchers. The venture's water stockpiling and circulation foundation will assist with relieving the effect of dry seasons by guaranteeing a consistent water supply during dry periods.

Ecological Effect: The venture has been planned in light of natural supportability. It incorporates arrangements for water reusing and re-energizing groundwater springs, which will assist with keeping up with environmental equilibrium and protect normal biological systems.

Between State Collaboration: The Kaleshwaram Venture likewise features the significance of between state participation in water asset the board. The Godavari Stream moves through different states, and compelling coordination is fundamental to guarantee evenhanded water circulation and resolve likely debates.

Difficulties and Concerns:

Natural Effect: The broad organization of channels and supplies affects nearby biological systems, remembering the uprooting of untamed life and changes for groundwater levels.

Monetary Expenses: The task's gigantic expense has brought up issues about its drawn out monetary maintainability, particularly given the huge energy costs related with lifting and moving water.

Between State Debates: Water-imparting questions to adjoining states, especially Andhra Pradesh and Maharashtra, have presented difficulties to the undertaking's smooth execution. Settling these debates is critical for its prosperity.

Activity and Upkeep: The powerful activity and support of the perplexing foundation network are indispensable for guaranteeing the venture's drawn out progress. Appropriate administration will be fundamental to forestall spillages, water misfortunes, and hardware breakdowns.

1. **Brief overview of the Kaleshwaram Project**

   The Kaleshwaram Lift Water system Task, a designing wonder arranged in the Indian province of Telangana, addresses one of the most aggressive and significant water asset the executives tries as of late. Introduced in June 2019, the undertaking gets its name from the town of Kaleshwaram, a position of strict importance where Ruler Shiva is loved. Intended to saddle the waters of the Godavari Stream, the venture includes an immense organization of trenches, siphon houses, repositories, and pipelines, with an expected expense surpassing Rs. 80,000 crore (around 11 billion USD). This multi-reason lift water system conspire holds the possibility to alter the financial scene of Telangana and then some.

   Key to the Kaleshwaram Undertaking's usefulness are its 20 decisively found siphon houses, each outfitted with a variety of high-limit siphons. These siphon houses assume a vital part in lifting water from the Godavari Stream to supplies and channels, empowering the proficient dissemination of water across immense districts. This broad organization guarantees a consistent and solid inventory of water over time, making it a unique advantage for a district that has generally wrestled with water shortage.

The task's repositories and tanks act as basic parts of its foundation, filling the double need of putting away and disseminating the redirected water. These repositories go about as a cradle, controlling the progression of water and guaranteeing a predictable stockpile for farming and homegrown use. By relieving occasional changes and tending to the difficulties of dry season, they give a help to ranchers and networks subject to horticulture and water assets.

Extending across large number of kilometers, the Kaleshwaram Task's tremendous arrangement of channels and pipelines befuddles Telangana, arriving at even the remotest regions. This many-sided network works with the productive transportation and designation of water, empowering both country and metropolitan areas to profit from the undertaking's water assets. It carries a recharged desire to horticulture, industry, and metropolitan improvement by guaranteeing fair admittance to this valuable asset. The effect of the Kaleshwaram Venture stretches out past the domain of horticulture. It can possibly invigorate monetary improvement on a critical scale. With a reliable water supply set up, ventures, for example, materials, food handling, and assembling are ready to flourish. This, thusly, converts into work creation and a general lift to the state's

economy. As ventures thrive and country livelihoods rise, the undertaking catalyzes a groundbreaking financial change.

Past its financial ramifications, the task resolves quite possibly of the most major problem in the locale — admittance to perfect and solid drinking water. By and large, water shortage has brought about various difficulties connected with general wellbeing and prosperity. The Kaleshwaram Undertaking's obligation to giving drinking water supply to country and metropolitan regions vows to upgrade the personal satisfaction for a huge number of inhabitants, adding to further developed wellbeing results and a superior way of life.

Besides, the Kaleshwaram Undertaking represents a devotion to ecological manageability. In its plan and execution, the undertaking consolidates measures to limit its biological impression. This incorporates water reusing and drives to re-energize groundwater springs, which assist with keeping up with biological equilibrium and protect normal biological systems, exhibiting a promise to blending human improvement with ecological conservation.

In any case, the undertaking isn't without its portion of difficulties and concerns. The broad framework organization, including waterways and repositories, possibly affects nearby environments, especially as far as natural life dislodging and changes in groundwater levels. Also, the task's enormous monetary expense has started conversations about its drawn out financial suitability, given the significant energy costs related with lifting and moving water. Settling between state water-sharing questions, especially with adjoining states like Andhra Pradesh and Maharashtra, stays a basic test that should be addressed for the task to flawlessly work. Finally, the compelling activity and upkeep of the mind boggling foundation organization will be foremost in forestalling spillages, water misfortunes, and gear breakdowns.

2. Importance in the context of Indian water infrastructure

Water is a valuable and crucial asset, and with regards to India, a country with a different environment, broad horticulture, and a prospering populace, it holds vital significance. The meaning of water in Indian water framework couldn't possibly be more significant, as it assumes a crucial part in supporting life, driving monetary development, and tending to the perplexing difficulties of water shortage, contamination, and environmental change.

Agribusiness and Food Security:

Farming is the foundation of India's economy, utilizing a huge piece of the populace. The accessibility of water is critical for crop development, and a significant part of the country's horticultural result depends on precipitation or water system. In this unique

situation, water foundation, like dams, channels, and repositories, assumes a basic part. These infrastructural components empower proficient capacity and circulation of water for water system, making it conceivable to develop crops consistently, even in areas with flighty precipitation designs. With India's consistently developing populace, guaranteeing food security stays a main concern, and water foundation is critical to accomplishing this objective.

Hydropower Age:

India's water framework contributes fundamentally to its energy area through hydropower age. Dams and supplies are fundamental parts of hydropower projects, outfitting the expected energy of streaming water to deliver power. These undertakings not just give a perfect and sustainable wellspring of energy yet in addition help in decreasing ozone harming substance discharges, adding to India's endeavors to battle environmental change. Besides, hydropower ventures can improve the energy security of the country by broadening its energy sources.

Modern Development:

India's expanding modern area vigorously depends on water for different cycles, including assembling, cooling, and waste treatment. Satisfactory water foundation guarantees a solid and feasible stockpile of water for ventures. Furthermore, effective wastewater treatment offices are essential to forestall modern contamination and safeguard the climate. Water framework upholds modern development and helps in the production of occupations and financial turn of events.

Urbanization and Drinking Water Supply:

As India goes through fast urbanization, the interest for clean savoring water urban areas and towns has flooded. Dependable water framework is fundamental to give consumable water to metropolitan populaces.

Water treatment plants, pipelines, and appropriation networks are essential parts of metropolitan water supply frameworks. Guaranteeing admittance to safe drinking water works on general wellbeing as well as adds to the general prosperity of metropolitan inhabitants.

Moderating Water Shortage:

Water shortage is a major problem in India, exacerbated by variables like populace development, changing weather conditions, and over-extraction of groundwater. Viable water framework, including water storage spaces, proficient water system frameworks, and water reusing instruments, can assist with relieving the effect of water shortage. Water collecting, for example, is an economical practice that, when coordinated into

foundation arranging, can expand water accessibility, particularly in water-pushed districts.

Natural Protection:

India's rich biodiversity and interesting biological systems rely upon the accessibility and nature of water. Appropriately oversaw water framework can assist with keeping up with environmental equilibrium and protect normal living spaces. Wetlands, streams, and lakes are fundamental environments that help different verdure as well as offer different biological types of assistance, including flood control, groundwater re-energize, and water sanitization. Interests in water foundation ought to incorporate measures to secure and reestablish these imperative biological systems.

Environmental Change Versatility:

India is progressively powerless against the effects of environmental change, including adjusted precipitation designs, increasing temperatures, and more successive outrageous climate occasions. Water foundation that integrates environment strength measures is vital for address these difficulties. For instance, developing versatile banks and flood control frameworks can assist with shielding networks from the overwhelming impacts of floods, which are turning out to be more successive and extreme.

Challenges and Economical Practices

Maturing Framework: A large number of India's current water foundation offices are maturing and needing support and modernization.

Water Contamination: Modern and metropolitan releases, as well as farming spillover, add to water contamination, requiring further developed wastewater treatment and contamination control measures.

Between State Water Questions: India's streams move through various states, frequently prompting arguments about water sharing, underscoring the requirement for powerful between state collaboration and water the executives instruments.

Ecological Effect: Enormous scope water foundation projects, like dams and repositories, can have unfavorable natural effects, including territory annihilation and modified stream environments. Feasible practices and ecological effect evaluations are vital to alleviate these impacts.

Chapter 2

The Genesis of Kaleshwaram

The Kaleshwaram Lift Water system Venture, situated in the Indian territory of Telangana, is a huge designing wonder that stands as a demonstration of human resourcefulness and assurance in tending to complex water difficulties. Spreading over a large number of kilometers and including a tremendous organization of waterways, siphon houses, pipelines, and supplies, the venture's beginning is a story of visionary initiative, mechanical development, and the mission for supportable turn of events. This thorough investigation dives into the authentic scenery, the pioneers behind its beginning, the designing complexities, between state participation, ecological contemplations, and the expected financial and social effect of the Kaleshwaram Venture.

Verifiable Setting

The verifiable setting of the Kaleshwaram Venture is established in the persistent water shortage that has tormented the Telangana area for quite a long time. With its semi-bone-dry environment and flighty precipitation designs, Telangana confronted repeating dry spells that injured agribusiness, impacted jobs, and prompted water-related trouble. The locale's reliance on the Godavari Stream was ruined by an absence of foundation to successfully tackle its waters. This section dives into the authentic water difficulties in Telangana and the locale's weakness to water shortage.

Visionary Initiative

The beginning of the Kaleshwaram Undertaking can be ascribed to visionary pioneers who perceived the capability of the Godavari Stream to change Telangana's fortunes. One such pioneer is K. Chandrashekar Rao, the Central Pastor of Telangana, whose steadfast obligation to the task focused on it for the state. This section investigates the job of visionary administration in considering and advocating the Kaleshwaram Task, stressing the political will and assurance expected to attempt such an aggressive undertaking.

Designing Wonder

The preparation and execution of the Kaleshwaram Undertaking address a noteworthy designing accomplishment. The task's intricacy is faltering, including a tremendous organization of trenches, siphon houses, pipelines, and supplies. The main point is to redirect water from the Godavari Stream and disseminate it to different locales in Telangana, guaranteeing solid water system, drinking water supply, and modern use. This part dives into the multifaceted designing subtleties of the task, featuring the inventive arrangements and careful arranging expected to carry it to completion.

Between State Collaboration

The Godavari Stream moves through numerous states, including Maharashtra and Andhra Pradesh, making between state participation critical for the venture's prosperity. This part investigates the elements of between state water-sharing arrangements, dealings, and the significance of impartial appropriation of water assets. The soul of participation and the difficulties looked in settling between state water questions are focal subjects in this section.

Natural Contemplations

Natural manageability is a basic part of the Kaleshwaram Task's beginning. Huge scope foundation projects like Kaleshwaram can possibly affect nearby environments and untamed life living spaces. This part talks about the consolidation of natural effect appraisals and moderation measures into the task's wanting to limit damage to the climate. Also, it investigates arrangements for water reusing and groundwater re-energize, lining up with standards of feasible water asset the executives.

Innovative Headways

One more vital consider the beginning of Kaleshwaram is the use of state of the art innovation. High level siphons, sensors, and mechanization frameworks are utilized in the siphon houses and along the channels to guarantee effective water the board and limit energy utilization. This section digs into the job of innovation in enhancing asset use and the mix of current developments into customary framework.

Financial and Social Effect

The possible financial and social effect of the Kaleshwaram Task is significant. By giving a steady and dependable water supply for water system, the venture is ready to help horticultural efficiency, increment food security, and improve rustic wages. The superior accessibility of water is supposed to invigorate modern development, make occupations, and add to the state's economy. Additionally, the venture tends to drinking water deficiencies, working on general wellbeing and prosperity in both country and

metropolitan regions. This part investigates the sweeping financial and social ramifications of the task.

Difficulties and Future Possibilities

In spite of its groundbreaking potential, the Kaleshwaram Task faces difficulties and concerns. The sheer monetary expense of the venture, assessed at over Rs. 80,000 crore, has brought up issues about its drawn out maintainability. The activity and upkeep of the broad foundation network are basic to forestall water misfortunes and guarantee its proceeded with usefulness. Also, tending to ecological worries and limiting the task's effect on nearby environments stay continuous difficulties. This part evaluates the difficulties and talks about expected future possibilities for the venture.

1. The Need for Water

Water, frequently alluded to as the remedy of life, is a crucial asset that supports all types of life on The planet. Its crucial significance rises above topographical, social, and cultural limits, as it assumes a principal part in human endurance, horticulture, industry, and the general strength of the planet. This article investigates the diverse requirement for water, accentuating its fundamental job in different parts of human life and natural maintainability.

1. **Endurance and Human Wellbeing:**
   Water is fundamental for human endurance. The human body is made out of around 60% water, and keeping up with sufficient hydration is basic for different physical processes. Water directs internal heat level, transports supplements and oxygen to cells, eliminates side-effects, and pads organs. Admittance to perfect and safe drinking water is major for forestalling waterborne sicknesses and guaranteeing general wellbeing. Lacking admittance to clean water can bring about waterborne ailments, hunger, and even demise, especially in districts with restricted admittance to disinfection and clean water sources.

2. **Horticulture and Food Security:**
   Water is the soul of agribusiness, the essential wellspring of food creation. Most of the world's freshwater assets are utilized for water system, empowering the development of yields that feed billions of individuals. Sufficient and dependable water supply is fundamental for crop development, and it assumes a critical part in accomplishing worldwide food security. Various rural practices, from downpour took care of cultivating to enormous scope water system projects, depend on water to deliver the grains, natural products, vegetables, and animals that structure the premise of our weight control plans.

3. **Industry and Monetary Development:**

The modern area relies upon water for a large number of cycles, including assembling, cooling, and waste treatment. Businesses like materials, gadgets, and mining depend intensely on water assets. A predictable and solid water supply is fundamental for modern development, work creation, and financial turn of events. Water likewise assumes a pivotal part in energy creation, as hydropower and cooling processes in nuclear energy stations require significant measures of water.

4. **Ecological Supportability:**

Water is a foundation of ecological maintainability. Sound amphibian environments, including streams, lakes, wetlands, and seas, support different verdure, giving biological system administrations, for example, water filtration, flood control, and natural surroundings for sea-going life. Reasonable water the board rehearses are fundamental to secure and protect these biological systems. Besides, water assets are personally associated with environment guideline, as they ingest and deliver heat, affecting atmospheric conditions and environment solidness.

5. **Environment Wellbeing:**

Freshwater environments are especially powerless against human exercises, including contamination, living space obliteration, and over-extraction of water assets. These effects can have crushing ramifications for oceanic biodiversity, disturb established pecking orders, and diminish the general strength of biological systems. Numerous types of fish, creatures of land and water, and waterfowl rely upon solid oceanic living spaces, making the assurance of water assets significant for saving biodiversity.

6. **Environmental Change Relief:**

Water assumes a part in relieving the impacts of environmental change. Timberlands and wetlands go about as carbon sinks, engrossing and putting away carbon dioxide from the climate. Water bodies like seas and oceans additionally ingest intensity and carbon dioxide, assisting with managing worldwide temperatures. Safeguarding these normal water-based frameworks is fundamental for environmental change moderation and transformation endeavors.

7. **Homegrown and Metropolitan Use:**
Water is irreplaceable for day to day homegrown and civil exercises. Past drinking, water is required for cooking, washing, cleaning, and sterilization. Admittance to perfect and safe drinking water isn't just fundamental for individual prosperity yet additionally a common freedom perceived by the Unified Countries. In metropolitan regions, civil
water supply frameworks guarantee admittance to consumable water for a great many occupants, adding to general wellbeing and metropolitan turn of events.

8. **Sporting and Stylish Worth:**

Water has innate sporting and tasteful worth. Lakes, waterways, sea shores, and repositories offer open doors for recreation, the travel industry, and social exercises. These normal water bodies give spaces to unwinding, sports, and happiness regarding the outside. Furthermore, the tasteful excellence of water highlights in scenes has enlivened workmanship, writing, and human imagination since the beginning of time.

1. **Droughts and water scarcity in Telangana**
Telangana, quite possibly of India's most youthful state, has generally wrestled with the difficulties of dry seasons and water shortage. Situated in the semi-parched Deccan Level, the area's environment is portrayed by high temperatures, flighty precipitation designs, and delayed droughts. The mix of these elements makes Telangana especially defenseless against water deficiencies, influencing agribusiness, jobs, and by and large personal satisfaction. This exposition digs into the causes, effects, and possible answers for address dry seasons and water shortage in Telangana.

Reasons for Water Shortage and Dry spells in Telangana:

Flighty Precipitation: Telangana encounters sporadic storm downpours, with varieties in timing and power. A postponed or lacking storm can bring about decreased water accessibility for crops and different purposes.

Over-Abuse of Groundwater: Over-dependence on groundwater for water system has prompted the exhaustion of springs in many pieces of the state. Unreasonable extraction of groundwater has brought down water tables and expanded the expense of siphoning water.

Wasteful Water The board: Obsolete and wasteful water system rehearses add to water wastage. Customary flood water system strategies are predominant in numerous areas, prompting huge water misfortunes.

Environmental Change: Changing environment designs have exacerbated the recurrence and force of dry seasons in Telangana. Increasing temperatures and adjusted precipitation designs have made the locale more helpless to water shortage.

Effects of Water Shortage and Dry seasons:

Horticultural Misfortunes: Agribusiness is the foundation of Telangana's economy, and water shortage straightforwardly influences crop yields. Dry seasons lead to trim disappointments, decreased rural earnings, and expanded obligation among ranchers.

Vocation Difficulties: The farming area gives work to a huge piece of the populace. Dry spells and water shortage bring about joblessness and misery movement, as ranchers and farming workers lose their occupations.

Drinking Water Deficiencies: Country and metropolitan regions the same face drinking water deficiencies during times of dry spell. Admittance to protected and clean drinking water turns into a basic concern, influencing general wellbeing.

Food Weakness: Marked down horticultural efficiency influences food accessibility and costs. Weak populaces might battle to bear or access nutritious food during seasons of shortage.

Monetary Effect: Water shortage upsets modern cycles, especially in water-concentrated areas. This can prompt decreased modern result, employment misfortunes, and financial precariousness.

Ecological Debasement: Dry seasons can prompt biological system stress, influencing neighborhood widely varied vegetation. Over-extraction of groundwater can bring about land subsidence and living space obliteration.

Endeavors to Address Water Shortage and Dry spells:

Water Protection: Advancing water preservation rehearses is fundamental to alleviate water shortage. Water reaping, water reusing, and effective water system techniques can assist with rationing water assets.

Groundwater Re-energize: Re-energizing springs through counterfeit re-energize structures and advancing capable groundwater use are pivotal for renewing exhausted groundwater levels.

Crop Expansion: Empowering ranchers to broaden their yields, including dry season safe assortments, can lessen water interest and improve flexibility to dry spells.

Proficient Water system: Progressing to current water system procedures, for example, dribble water system and sprinkler frameworks can fundamentally decrease water wastage in agribusiness.

Dry spell Readiness and Alleviation: Growing early admonition frameworks, alternate courses of action, and help measures for dry season impacted networks is crucial for limiting the effects of dry seasons.

Between State Participation: Teaming up with adjoining states to oversee shared stream assets and resolve water-sharing debates is fundamental for evenhanded water dispersion.

Environment Tough Horticulture: Advancing environment strong rural works on, including the utilization of dry season safe yield assortments and agroforestry, can upgrade farming supportability.

Strategy Changes: Carrying out approaches that empower maintainable water the board, direct groundwater extraction, and boost water-effective practices is vital for long haul water security.

2. Agricultural challenges and socio-economic implications

Agribusiness is the foundation of numerous economies around the world, giving food, jobs, and unrefined components for various ventures. In any case, horticulture faces a large group of difficulties that influence food creation as well as have critical financial ramifications. This article investigates the critical agrarian difficulties and their extensive effects on social orders and economies.

Farming Difficulties:

Environmental Change: Environmental change achieves unusual weather conditions, including outrageous intensity, dry seasons, floods, and changing precipitation levels. These elements disturb planting and gathering seasons, decrease crop yields, and increment the predominance of irritations and illnesses.

Water Shortage: Water shortage is a squeezing challenge in numerous rural locales. Over-extraction of groundwater, wasteful water system practices, and rivalry for water assets among different areas add to this issue. Absence of admittance to solid water sources influences crop creation and animals the board.

Land Debasement: Soil disintegration, supplement exhaustion, and land corruption are main pressing issues. Impractical agrarian practices, deforestation, and urbanization add to the deficiency of arable land. Debased soils lessen rural efficiency and increment the gamble of yield disappointment.

Nuisances and Illnesses: Farming bugs and sicknesses, like bugs, organisms, and infections, can obliterate yields and animals. Environmental change can fuel these issues by adjusting the dissemination and conduct of irritations and microbes.

Market Access and Value Unpredictability: Restricted market access, combined with unstable product costs, makes it hard for ranchers to sell their produce at fair costs. This can bring about pay unsteadiness and beat interests in farming down.

Financial Ramifications:

Food Security: Horticultural difficulties straightforwardly influence food security. Marked down crop yields, food value spikes, and dispersion interruptions can prompt food deficiencies and lack of healthy sustenance, influencing the prosperity of millions of individuals.

Rustic Livelihoods: Farming is an essential type of revenue for a huge number of individuals, particularly in provincial regions. Challenges like environmental change and market unpredictability undermine the vocations of ranchers and agrarian workers, prompting neediness and movement to metropolitan regions.

Financial Development: Horticulture contributes fundamentally to the Gross domestic product of numerous nations, especially in creating districts. Rural difficulties can obstruct monetary development, as decreased farming efficiency influences the actual area as well as enterprises subject to agribusiness.

Rustic Metropolitan Relocation: When agribusiness becomes unreasonable because of difficulties like water shortage and land corruption, country populaces frequently move to metropolitan regions looking for elective vocations. This relocation can strain metropolitan foundation and administrations while adding to social and monetary differences.

Ecological Debasement: Unreasonable rural practices can prompt natural corruption, including deforestation, soil disintegration, and contamination. These issues hurt biological systems as well as have long haul financial outcomes by influencing water quality, biodiversity, and environment administrations.

Wellbeing and Sustenance: Agrarian difficulties can affect the accessibility and moderateness of nutritious food sources. Diminished crop yields and pay insecurity can prompt deficient eating regimens and hunger, especially among weak populaces.

Social Security: Financial difficulties in farming can prompt social shakiness. Ranchers confronting monetary misery might turn to fights, exhibitions, or even land-related clashes, presenting difficulties to social union and political solidness.

Moderation and Transformation Systems:

Environment Versatile Horticulture: Advancing environment strong cultivating rehearses, like dry season safe yield assortments and preservation agribusiness, can assist ranchers with adjusting to changing environment conditions.

Feasible Water The executives: Carrying out proficient water system frameworks, further developing water use effectiveness, and advancing practical groundwater the board can address water shortage in farming.

Soil Preservation: Soil protection methods, for example, terracing, reforestation, and harvest turn, can battle land debasement and upgrade soil fruitfulness.

Incorporated Irritation The executives: Coordinated bother the board techniques that lessen pesticide use and advance regular vermin control strategies can alleviate bug and sickness challenges.

Market Access and Value Adjustment: Growing business sector access for ranchers, further developing inventory network foundation, and executing cost adjustment measures can improve the financial states of ranchers.

Expansion: Empowering crop broadening and elective pay sources, for example, agroforestry and domesticated animals the executives, can lessen the dependence on a solitary yield or animals species.

Examination and Advancement: Putting resources into agrarian exploration and advancement is significant for growing new innovations, crop assortments, and practices that can address horticultural difficulties really.

B. The Visionary Behind It

Visionary pioneers are people who have the prescience, assurance, and innovativeness to graph a course for the future that changes social orders, enterprises, or associations.

Their capacity to imagine a superior tomorrow and rouse others to go along with them on that excursion is a sign of their initiative. In this article, we will investigate the characteristics and effect of visionary pioneers, drawing motivation from outstanding figures who have made a permanent imprint on history.

Characteristics of a Visionary Chief:

Prescience: Visionary pioneers have the capacity to expect future patterns, difficulties, and open doors. They see what others may not and can conceptualize an alternate reality.

Boldness: It takes fortitude to seek after a dream that rocks the boat or faces resistance. Visionary pioneers will face challenges and endure analysis chasing their objectives.

Advancement: Visionaries are many times trailblazers of development. They present novel thoughts, advancements, or approaches that disturb laid out standards and drive progress.

Energy: Enthusiasm powers a visionary chief's commitment to their vision. It moves them to drive forward, in any event, when confronted with misfortunes or obstructions.

Relational abilities: Successful correspondence is fundamental for passing a dream on to other people. Visionary pioneers can express their thoughts in a convincing manner, motivating others to go along with them.

Sympathy: Understanding the necessities and yearnings of others is essential for accumulating support. Visionary pioneers identify with individuals they lead and look for arrangements that benefit everyone's benefit.

Prominent Visionary Pioneers:

Mahatma Gandhi: Mahatma Gandhi's vision of peaceful common noncompliance assumed a crucial part in India's battle for freedom from English provincial rule. His obligation to equity, balance, and tranquil obstruction motivated millions and left a persevering through inheritance.

Nelson Mandela: Nelson Mandela's vision of a free and popularity based South Africa, where racial correspondence won, directed his initiative during the destroying of politically-sanctioned racial segregation. His flexibility and limit with regards to absolution keep on motivating the world.

Martin Luther Lord Jr.: Dr. Martin Luther Lord Jr. had a fantasy of racial fairness and social equality for all Americans. His strong addresses and resolute obligation to peaceful dissent were instrumental in propelling the social equality development in the US.

Steve Occupations: Steve Occupations, fellow benefactor of Mac Inc., was a visionary in the realm of innovation and plan. His vision of easy to use, delightfully planned, and inventive items changed enterprises and made Apple a worldwide force to be reckoned with.

Elon Musk: Elon Musk is a cutting edge visionary pioneer known for his aggressive objectives in space investigation, environmentally friendly power, and electric vehicles. His organizations, including SpaceX and Tesla, are at the bleeding edge of mechanical advancement.

Effect of Visionary Initiative:

Social Change: Visionary pioneers have the ability to light friendly change. Their backing for equity, equity, and basic freedoms has reshaped social orders and establishments.

Advancement and Progress: Visionary pioneers drive development and innovative advancement. They present noteworthy thoughts and advances that meaningfully alter the manner in which we live and work.

Motivation: Visionary pioneers act as a wellspring of motivation for people and networks. Their accounts and achievements rouse others to seek after their fantasies and have a beneficial outcome.

Inheritance: The tradition of visionary pioneers perseveres through lengthy after their time. Their thoughts and standards keep on molding the world and impact people in the future.

Worldwide Effect: Numerous visionary chiefs have a worldwide effect. Their thoughts and drives rise above borders, resolving issues that influence mankind overall, for example, environmental change, neediness, and common liberties.

Challenges Looked by Visionary Pioneers:

Protection from Change: Visionary pioneers frequently face opposition from the people who are alright with business as usual. Conquering this obstruction can be a critical test.

Analysis and Resistance: Seeking after a strong vision can prompt analysis and resistance from different quarters. Visionary pioneers should have the strength to endure such difficulties.

Intricacy: A few dreams are mind boggling and diverse, requiring fastidious preparation and execution. Dealing with the complexities of a dream can plague.

Adjusting Partner Interests: Visionary pioneers should explore the interests of different partners, including state run administrations, organizations, and common society, to understand their objectives.

1. Key figures and leaders involved

Groundbreaking drives, whether in legislative issues, science, industry, or social developments, frequently depend on the vision and administration of key figures who drive change, move others, and shape the course of history. In this exposition, we will investigate the jobs and commitments of a few unmistakable pioneers and figures who play played urgent parts in extraordinary drives across different spaces.

1. Mahatma Gandhi:

Mahatma Gandhi, a transcending figure in India's battle for autonomy, is eminent for his way of thinking of peaceful opposition, or "Satyagraha." Gandhi's initiative and unflinching obligation to peacefulness roused millions and assumed a basic part in India's battle for independence from English pioneer rule. His common insubordination developments, including the Salt Walk and Quit India Development, activated the majority and caused global to notice India's objective. Gandhi's vision of a free and confident India directed the country's way to freedom in 1947.

2. **Martin Luther Ruler Jr.:**

Dr. Martin Luther Ruler Jr. was a critical forerunner in the American social equality development during the mid-twentieth 100 years. His vision of a racially incorporated and just society drove the social equality progress ahead. Ruler's strong discourses, including his notorious "I Have a Fantasy" discourse, stirred help for integration, casting a ballot rights, and fairness for African Americans. His initiative and obligation to

peaceful dissent prompted critical administrative changes, including the Social equality Demonstration of 1964 and the Democratic Privileges Demonstration of 1965.

3. **Marie Curie:**

Marie Curie, a spearheading researcher in the mid twentieth 100 years, made groundbreaking commitments to the fields of material science and science. She was the primary lady to win a Nobel Prize and stays the main individual to have gotten Nobel Prizes in two different logical fields (Physical science and Science). Curie's weighty examination on radioactivity established the groundwork for progresses in atomic physical science and clinical diagnostics. Her vision for logical revelation and her devotion to her work have made a permanent imprint on mainstream researchers.

4. **Nelson Mandela:**

Nelson Mandela, South Africa's most memorable dark president, was a focal figure in the development to destroy politically-sanctioned racial segregation, an arrangement of regulated racial isolation and separation. Mandela's vision of a unified, vote based, and nonracial South Africa propelled individuals all over the planet. He burned through 27 years in jail for his enemy of politically-sanctioned racial segregation activism however arose as an image of compromise and pardoning. Mandela's initiative and obligation to serene discussion prompted the finish of politically-sanctioned racial segregation and the introduction of another South Africa.

5. **Steve Occupations:**

Steve Occupations, fellow benefactor of Macintosh Inc., was a visionary forerunner in the innovation business. His vision of easy to understand, wonderfully planned, and imaginative items changed the manner in which individuals communicate with innovation. Occupations assumed a urgent part in the improvement of famous items like the iPhone, iPad, and MacBook. His capacity to expect customer requirements and his firm quest for greatness left a getting through heritage in the realm of shopper hardware and plan.

6. **Malala Yousafzai:**

Malala Yousafzai, Pakistani training dissident, turned into a worldwide image of young ladies' schooling and ladies' freedoms. Malala's vision for widespread training and her valiant support acquired her the Nobel Harmony Prize at 17 years old, making her the most youthful beneficiary ever. Regardless of being designated by the Taliban for her activism, Malala keeps on advocating the right to schooling for young ladies around the world.

7. **Elon Musk:**

Elon Musk is a contemporary visionary pioneer known for his aggressive objectives in space investigation, environmentally friendly power, and electric vehicles. Musk's organizations, including SpaceX, Tesla, and SolarCity, are at the cutting edge of mechanical development. His vision of a maintainable future with electric vehicles, sun powered energy, and the colonization of Mars drives his work and rouses progressions in the aviation and auto ventures.

8. **Greta Thunberg:**

Greta Thunberg, a Swedish natural extremist, has turned into a main voice in the worldwide development to battle environmental change. Her vision of earnest environment activity and her assurance to consider world pioneers responsible have stirred great many youngsters around the world. Thunberg's "Fridays for Future" school strike development has ignited environment fights and strategy changes across the globe.

9. **Dr. Anthony Fauci:**

Dr. Anthony Fauci, a noticeable immunologist and overseer of the Public Organization of Sensitivity and Irresistible Illnesses (NIAID) in the US, plays had a basic impact in answering general wellbeing emergencies, including the HIV/Helps pandemic and the Coronavirus pandemic. His vision of proof based, science-driven general wellbeing estimates has been instrumental in directing the country's reaction to irresistible illnesses.

10. **Angela Merkel:**

Angela Merkel, the previous Chancellor of Germany, is perceived for her administration in the European Association and her part in dealing with the Eurozone emergency. Merkel's vision of a unified and financially stable Europe directed her initiative during a difficult period for the EU. Her logical way to deal with strategy and administration gained her worldwide appreciation and impact.

Effect and Heritage:

These vital figures and pioneers significantly affect their individual fields and on society in general. Their visionary administration, whether in the domains of legislative issues, science, innovation, or civil rights, has molded the course of history and enlivened positive change. Their heritages proceed to impact and guide the activities of current and people in the future, featuring the getting through force of vision and authority in driving extraordinary drives.

2. Political and environmental considerations

The interchange among legislative issues and the climate is a mind boggling and dynamic relationship that has significant ramifications for the prosperity of social orders and the wellbeing of the planet. Political choices and approaches can altogether influence the climate, and alternately, natural issues can shape political plans. In this paper, we will investigate the perplexing snare of political and natural contemplations, the difficulties they present, and the basic for compelling and supportable arrangements.

Political Contemplations:

Strategy and Guideline: Political choices assume a significant part in forming natural approach and guideline. Legislatures authorize regulations and guidelines that oversee issues, for example, contamination control, land use, and normal asset the board.

Monetary Interests: Financial contemplations frequently impact political choices in regards to the climate. Businesses that depend on petroleum derivatives, mining, and assembling might oppose guidelines that limit their exercises because of monetary worries.

Worldwide Relations: Natural issues have worldwide ramifications, and political pioneers take part in peaceful accords and arrangements to address them. Arrangements like the Paris Settlement on environmental change epitomize the significance of tact in handling natural difficulties.

General Assessment: Public discernment and assessment on ecological issues can influence political choices. Chosen authorities frequently answer the worries and requests of their constituents, especially with regards to issues like air and water quality.

Asset Distribution: Political pioneers should come to conclusions about how to designate assets, including financing for ecological insurance, protection endeavors, and calamity reaction. Monetary requirements can influence ecological drives.

Ecological Contemplations:

Environmental Change: Environmental change is quite possibly of the most squeezing natural test. Increasing worldwide temperatures, ocean level ascent, and outrageous climate occasions have expansive ramifications for biological systems, economies, and social orders.

Biodiversity Misfortune: Human exercises, like deforestation and living space annihilation, add to the deficiency of biodiversity. The elimination of species can disturb environments and have flowing consequences for natural pecking orders and biological systems.

Asset Exhaustion: The unreasonable utilization of regular assets, including water, fisheries, and timberlands, can prompt asset consumption. This can compromise the accessibility of fundamental assets for people in the future.

Contamination: Contamination from modern, farming, and metropolitan sources can taint air, water, and soil. Contamination unfavorably affects human wellbeing, biological systems, and biodiversity.

Biological system Administrations: Environments offer basic types of assistance, including water refinement, fertilization, and environment guideline. Ecological contemplations include safeguarding these administrations to keep up with human prosperity.

Challenges in Adjusting Political and Ecological Contemplations:

Momentary versus Long haul Interests: Political pioneers frequently face strain to address transient monetary and political needs, which might struggle with long haul ecological manageability objectives.

Financial Interests: Monetary interests, especially those related with businesses that have unfavorable ecological effects, can apply huge impact over political navigation, making it trying to order harmless to the ecosystem approaches.

Worldwide Coordination: Ecological issues frequently require global participation and coordination. Political conflicts and contending interests among countries can hinder successful worldwide reactions to natural difficulties.

Public Mindfulness and Commitment: Building public mindfulness and backing for natural issues can be a sluggish and testing process. Policymakers should explore public feeling and answer public requests.

Compelling Techniques for Tending to Political and Ecological Contemplations:

Proof Based Arrangement: Leaders ought to put together strategies with respect to sound logical proof and information to guarantee that ecological contemplations are enough tended to.

Partner Commitment: Drawing in with different partners, including ecological supporters, industry delegates, and impacted networks, can prompt more adjusted and powerful strategies.

Long haul Arranging: Policymakers ought to focus on long haul manageability over transient increases, taking into account the prosperity of people in the future.

Worldwide Participation: Cooperative endeavors among countries are critical for tending to worldwide ecological difficulties like environmental change. Political pioneers ought to effectively take part in worldwide exchanges and arrangements.

Motivators and Guidelines: States can utilize a blend of impetuses and guidelines to advance harmless to the ecosystem practices and ventures.

Contextual investigation: The Paris Understanding

The Paris Settlement on environmental change is a great representation of the crossing point among political and ecological contemplations. Taken on in 2015, the understanding addresses a worldwide obligation to battle environmental change and breaking point an Earth-wide temperature boost to well under 2 degrees Celsius above pre-modern levels.

Political pioneers from around the world met up to arrange and settle on the Paris Understanding, perceiving the earnest requirement for aggregate activity on environmental change. This notable accord mirrors the acknowledgment that natural contemplations should rise above political limits and financial interests.

The Paris Understanding shows the force of political will and worldwide participation in resolving squeezing natural issues. Notwithstanding, its viability at last depends on the responsibility and activities of individual countries to satisfy their vows.

3 |

Chapter 3

Engineering Marvel

Designing wonders are remarkable accomplishments of human creativity and development that push the limits of what is conceivable. These remarkable accomplishments length many disciplines, from common and primary designing to aviation and innovation. Since forever ago, these wonders have not just shown our capacity to conquer complex difficulties yet have additionally changed social orders, economies, and our comprehension of the world. In this investigation of designing wonders, we will dig into probably the most notorious and pivotal models, their importance, and the enduring effect they have had on our reality.1. The Incomparable

Pyramids of Giza: Stupendous Authority

The Incomparable Pyramids of Giza, situated on the Giza Level in Egypt, are among the most notorious designing wonders in mankind's set of experiences. Worked during the Old Realm time of antiquated Egypt, these giant designs have represented north of 4,500 years. The biggest of the pyramids, the Pyramid of Khufu (otherwise called the Pyramid of Cheops), is an astonishing building accomplishment, containing over 2.3 million limestone obstructs, each gauging a few tons.

These pyramids filled in as burial places for Pharaohs and contained unpredictable ways, chambers, and entombment chambers. The accuracy with which the pyramids were developed is a demonstration of the high level designing information on the old Egyptians. The Incomparable Pyramid, specifically, is well known for its close ideal arrangement with the cardinal places of the compass.

The meaning of the Incomparable Pyramids stretches out past their design wonder. They address the resourcefulness of old civic establishments and keep on being a wellspring of interest and secret, starting various logical requests and investigations.

2. The Panama Waterway: Crossing over Mainlands

The Panama Waterway is a wonderful accomplishment of designing that changed worldwide exchange and route. Finished in 1914, this 50-mile-long stream associates the Atlantic and Pacific Seas, permitting boats to sidestep the tricky and extended journey around the southern tip of South America. The trench comprises of an

arrangement of locks and entryways that raise and lower vessels, empowering them to navigate the fluctuating rises of the Isthmus of Panama.

The effect of the Panama Waterway on worldwide trade couldn't possibly be more significant. It has decisively diminished travel distances, brought down delivery costs, and worked with the development of products between the Eastern and Western Sides of the equator. The channel's development was a great endeavor that included defeating considerable designing difficulties, including the removal of immense measures of earth and the making of the Gatun Lake, one of the world's biggest counterfeit lakes.

3. The Global Space Station: Mankind's Home in Circle

The Global Space Station (ISS) addresses a cooperative exertion including different nations and space organizations, including NASA, Roscosmos, ESA, JAXA, and CSA. Circling roughly 250 miles above Earth, the ISS fills in as a space lab and a stage for logical exploration and global participation.

This designing wonder is a demonstration of the capacities of human space investigation. It comprises of interconnected modules, research facilities, and living quarters that are persistently possessed by space travelers from different countries. The ISS conducts tests in fields like physical science, science, stargazing, and medication, adding to how we might interpret space and propelling innovation for future space missions.

The ISS embodies the potential for global collaboration chasing after logical disclosure and investigation past Earth's limits.

4. The Channel Passage: Connecting England and France

The Channel Passage, frequently alluded to as the Eurotunnel or Chunnel, is a designing victory that interfaces the Unified Realm and France underneath the English Channel. This 31.4-mile burrow, which incorporates both rail and administration burrows, works with the transportation of travelers and cargo between the two nations.

Finished in 1994, the Channel Passage remains as an image of cross-line coordinated effort and development. Its development included the boring of passages through layers of chalk and earth underneath the seabed, all while planning exact arrangement between the French and English burrowing crews.

The Channel Passage significantly affects transportation and exchange, empowering productive rail travel and the consistent development of merchandise between the European landmass and the UK.

5. The Hoover Dam: Outfitting the Force of the Colorado Stream

The Hoover Dam, a titanic substantial curve gravity dam on the Colorado Stream, is a striking instance of designing greatness. Finished in 1936 during the Economic crisis of the early 20s, the dam serves different capabilities, including flood control, water capacity, and hydroelectric power age.

The dam's development required the position of over 3.25 million cubic yards of concrete, a gigantic endeavor that changed the rough Colorado Stream scene. The dam's supply, Lake Mead, is perhaps of the biggest man-made lake in the US and gives fundamental water assets toward the southwestern states.

Notwithstanding its utilitarian purposes, the Hoover Dam has turned into a notorious image of American designing and a famous traveler objective.

6. The Burj Khalifa: Aiming high

The Burj Khalifa, situated in Dubai, Joined Bedouin Emirates, is the tallest man-made structure on the planet. Remaining at a stunning level of 2,722 feet (829.8 meters) and containing 163 stories, the Burj Khalifa is a design wonder that exhibits human innovativeness and designing ability.

Planned by the prestigious modeler Adrian Smith, the Burj Khalifa highlights an unmistakable ventured plan enlivened by Islamic design. Its development included progressed designing strategies, including the utilization of high-strength concrete, a creative lift framework, and a modern cooling framework to battle the outrageous desert heat.

The Burj Khalifa fills in as a demonstration of the aggressive vision of Dubai and its obligation to pushing the limits of design and designing accomplishment.

7. The Huge Hadron Collider: Unwinding the Secrets of the Universe

The Huge Hadron Collider (LHC), situated underneath the Franco-Swiss line at CERN (the European Association for Atomic Exploration), is the world's most impressive atom smasher. This gigantic machine comprises of a 17-mile (27-kilometer) round burrow, in which protons are advanced rapidly to almost the speed of light prior to impacting.

The LHC's basic role is to research key inquiries regarding the universe, like the presence of the Higgs boson and the idea of dull matter and dim energy. Its analyses have extended how we might interpret molecule physical science and the basic powers that administer the universe.

The designing behind the LHC is a wonder in itself, including superconducting magnets, vacuum frameworks, and complex locators. It addresses a demonstration of worldwide joint effort chasing logical information.

8. The Brilliant Entryway Scaffold: Symbol of San Francisco

The Brilliant Entryway Extension, a famous engineered overpass crossing the Brilliant Door Waterway in San Francisco, California, is praised for its staggering plan and designing tastefulness. At the point when it was finished in 1937, it was the longest and tallest engineered overpass on the planet.

Planned by engineer Joseph Strauss and modeler Irving Morrow, the Brilliant Entryway Scaffold includes an unmistakable Global Orange tone and ranges 4,200 feet (1,280 meters). Its development confronted testing conditions, major areas of strength for including, fierce waters, and thick haze.

Today, the Brilliant Door Scaffold remains as a getting through image of San Francisco and a demonstration of the imaginative soul of American designing and plan.

9. The Three Canyons Dam: Restraining China's Yangtze Waterway

The Three Crevasses Dam, arranged on the Yangtze Waterway in China, is one of the biggest hydroelectric power projects on the planet. This fantastic dam, finished in 2006, remains at 607 feet (185 meters) and stretches north of 7,500 feet (2,300 meters) long.

The dam's essential capabilities incorporate flood control, power age, and route enhancement for the Yangtze Waterway. It has a limit of more than 22,500 megawatts and gives power to a great many individuals in China.

The development of the Three Canyons Dam was a goliath undertaking that elaborate the movement of millions of individuals and the immersion of enormous areas of land. It addresses a huge accomplishment in enormous scope foundation improvement.

10. The Web: A Worldwide Data Insurgency

The web is one of the most extraordinary and persuasive designing wonders of the cutting edge period. It has changed correspondence, data dispersal, trade, and basically every part of present day life.

The web's starting points can be followed back to the ARPANET project in the last part of the 1960s, which looked to make a vigorous and decentralized network for military and scholarly purposes. Throughout the long term, it developed into a worldwide organization that interfaces billions of gadgets and clients around the world.

The web's foundation includes an intricate arrangement of switches, server farms, undersea links, and satellite organizations. Its effect on society has been significant,

cultivating globalization, empowering remote work and schooling, and democratizing admittance to data.

11. The Enormous Succinct Study Telescope: Looking into the Universe's Mysteries

The Huge Concise Review Telescope (LSST) is a momentous galactic observatory right now under development in Chile. Once functional, the LSST will review the whole southern sky at regular intervals, catching pictures of billions of systems, stars, and heavenly items.

The LSST's essential mission is to investigate and figure out the secrets of the universe, including dim matter and dim energy, supernovae, and the transient occasions that shape the universe. Its state of the art innovation, including a 3.2-gigapixel camera, will give a remarkable perspective on the night sky.

The LSST addresses the zenith of present day cosmic designing and will contribute fundamentally to how we might interpret the universe.

1. Design and Planning

Plan and arranging are essential cycles that shape the physical and practical parts of our assembled climate. From the format of urban communities and structures to the making of items and innovations, these cycles assume a critical part in deciding how we communicate with and experience our general surroundings. In this exposition, we will investigate the meaning of plan and arranging, their effect on different parts of our lives, and the key rules that support fruitful plan and arranging attempts.

The Pith of Plan and Arranging:

Configuration is the conscious and innovative flow of considering and making an answer for an issue or challenge. It incorporates a large number of disciplines, including engineering, modern plan, visual depiction, and client experience plan. A definitive objective of configuration is to enhance usefulness, style, and client experience while tending to explicit necessities and requirements.

Arranging, then again, is the methodical course of imagining, coordinating, and organizing different components to accomplish an ideal result. It frequently includes setting targets, distinguishing assets, and laying out timetables and methodology. Arranging is a basic part of powerful task the executives and is fundamental for accomplishing wanted objectives proficiently.

The Job of Plan and Arranging in Different Settings:

Metropolitan Preparation: Metropolitan organizers plan and plan urban areas and networks to enhance land use, transportation, framework, and public spaces. They

intend to make maintainable, open, and tastefully satisfying metropolitan conditions that improve the personal satisfaction for occupants.

Structural Plan: Draftsmen are answerable for planning structures that are useful, safe, and outwardly engaging. They consider factors like space use, energy productivity, and social importance in their plans.

Item Plan: Item creators make purchaser items that are both practical and stylishly satisfying. They center around client experience, ergonomics, and materials to plan items that address explicit issues and inclinations.

Visual depiction: Visual planners utilize visual components, typography, and design to pass on data and make visual characters for brands, associations, and distributions. They assume a urgent part in promoting and correspondence.

Transportation Arranging: Transportation organizers plan and plan transportation frameworks, including streets, public travel, and air terminals, to guarantee effective and safe development of individuals and products.

Ecological Preparation: Natural organizers work to limit the natural effect of improvement projects. They consider factors like supportability, protection, and asset the executives.

Standards of Fruitful Plan and Arranging:

Client Focused Approach: Successful plan and arranging focus on the necessities and inclinations of end-clients. Understanding client conduct and inclinations is vital to making arrangements that are instinctive and easy to use.

Usefulness: Plan and arranging ought to enhance usefulness to guarantee that the expected design is met proficiently. This requires a profound comprehension of the issue to be settled or the objective to be accomplished.

Feel: Visual allure is a significant part of plan, as style can impact how individuals see and collaborate with an item, space, or framework. Great plan makes progress toward both structure and capability.

Supportability: Feasible plan and arranging think about the drawn out influence on the climate and networks. It includes limiting asset utilization, decreasing waste, and relieving ecological damage.

Openness: Plan ought to be comprehensive, guaranteeing that items, spaces, and innovations are available to people with handicaps and various foundations. This guideline advances equivalent open doors and social value.

Productivity: Arranging looks to upgrade asset allotment and using time productively. Proficient arranging diminishes costs, improves efficiency, and limits delays.

Instances of Significant Plan and Arranging:

The High Line, New York City: The High Line is a raised metropolitan park based on a neglected railroad track. This inventive venture changed a neglected space into a dynamic recreational area, renewing the encompassing area and advancing economical metropolitan turn of events.

Curitiba's Transport Fast Travel Framework, Brazil: Curitiba's inventive BRT framework is a model of effective metropolitan preparation. It gives reasonable, quick transportation and has significantly decreased gridlock and contamination.

The iPhone: Apple's iPhone reformed the cell phone industry through its easy to understand plan, touchscreen interface, and consistent reconciliation of equipment and programming.

The Sydney Show House: Planned by draftsman Jørn Utzon, the Sydney Drama House is a notorious image of Australia. Its imaginative and unmistakable shell-like design has turned into a social milestone.

The Supportable City, Dubai: This arranged local area in Dubai centers around maintainability by consolidating sustainable power sources, green spaces, and effective transportation frameworks. It fills in as a model for supportable metropolitan turn of events.

Challenges in Plan and Arranging:

Adjusting Clashing Objectives: Plan and arranging frequently include compromises between various goals, like expense, usefulness, and supportability. Finding some kind of harmony can challenge.

Fast Mechanical Advances: Innovation is developing quickly, and originators and organizers should stay up with new instruments, materials, and developments.

Administrative Consistence: Undertakings should frequently comply to severe guidelines, codes, and principles, which can muddle the plan and arranging process.

Asset Requirements: Restricted assets, whether monetary, material, or human, can present huge difficulties in plan and arranging.

Complex Partner Association: Many undertakings include numerous partners with assorted interests, making coordination and agreement building testing.

1. **The intricacies of designing Kaleshwaram**

   The Kaleshwaram Lift Water system Task in the Indian province of Telangana remains as a demonstration of human designing and development. This aggressive undertaking, intended to address water shortage and upgrade horticultural efficiency in the locale, is a complicated snare of channels, repositories, and siphoning stations. In this exposition, we will dig into the complexities of planning the Kaleshwaram project, investigating its parts, targets, and the difficulties looked during its preparation and execution.

   The Specific circumstance: Water Shortage in Telangana

   Telangana, in the same way as other different locales in India, faces the common difficulties of water shortage and dry season. The state's overwhelmingly agrarian economy intensely relies upon water system for horticultural food. By and large, the locale has wrestled with lacking water assets, lopsided dissemination of precipitation, and the dependence on storm downpours.

   To address these difficulties and change the agrarian scene, the public authority of Telangana left on the Kaleshwaram Lift Water system Task. The task planned to tackle and proficiently deal with the Godavari Stream's water assets, giving a solid wellspring of water to dry spell inclined regions.

   Planning the Complicated Organization:

   Medigadda Flood: The Medigadda Torrent, worked across the Godavari Stream, fills in as the undertaking's beginning stage. It redirects stream water into a progression of channels for additional conveyance.

   Siphoning Stations: The core of the task lies in its siphoning stations. These stations are outfitted with huge siphons equipped for lifting water to fluctuating heights. The siphons assume a basic part in guaranteeing that water arrives at even the most noteworthy fields, a surprising accomplishment of designing.

Interface Waterways: An organization of connection channels befuddles the task region, interfacing the Godavari Stream to different repositories and dispersion focuses. These trenches are fastidiously intended to improve water stream and limit misfortunes because of vanishing and leakage.

Repositories: The Kaleshwaram project incorporates the development of a few supplies to store water during the rainstorm season and delivery it for water system during dry periods. These repositories give truly necessary water security to ranchers.

Lifts and Sumps: Lifts and sumps are fundamental parts that work with the exchange of water to various levels and dispersion focuses. These designs require exact designing to successfully deal with the progression of water.

Circulation Organization: The venture incorporates a broad conveyance network that conveys water to fields through a progression of trenches and sub-channels. This guarantees that water arrives at the farthest corners of the rural scene.

Challenges Looked in Plan and Execution:

Geological Variety: The task region includes a different scope of geological highlights, from fields to raised levels. Planning a framework that could proficiently circulate water across these differing territories required cautious preparation and designing.

Cost Contemplations: The task's gigantic scope and intricacy accompanied a significant monetary weight. Offsetting cost-viability with the requirement for a solid water supply was a key test.

Ecological Effect: Dealing with the natural effect of such a huge scope project is fundamental. Guaranteeing that the venture doesn't hurt environments, nearby vegetation, or water quality is a perplexing undertaking.

Highway Participation: The Godavari Stream moves through different Indian states, and the undertaking's water redirection raised worries among downstream states. Arranging highway arrangements and tending to worries was a vital part of the venture's preparation.

Specialized Mastery: Building and keeping up with the task's foundation required an elevated degree of specialized skill. Specialists and laborers confronted complex difficulties connected with water power, materials, and development.

Local area Commitment: The task impacted neighborhood networks, including those dislodged by repository development. Guaranteeing their interest, tending to worries, and giving recovery and pay were basic parts of the venture's execution.

Advantages and Future Ramifications:

Expanded Horticultural Efficiency: The venture has changed the rural scene of Telangana, furnishing ranchers with a solid wellspring of water for water system. This has prompted expanded crop yields and further developed livelihoods.

Dry spell Alleviation: By putting away and conveying water effectively, the undertaking has moderated the effect of dry seasons, guaranteeing that in any event, during dry periods, farming can flourish.

Financial Development: Further developed horticultural efficiency straightforwardly affects the state's economy, helping rustic salaries and encouraging monetary development.

Natural Supportability: The task consolidates measures to limit its natural effect, including water the board rehearses that think about biological maintainability.

Highway Participation: The effective execution of the undertaking required joint effort and discussion with adjoining states. This soul of participation starts a trend for tending to water-sharing issues in the district.

Future Development: The Kaleshwaram project fills in as an establishment for future extensions and improvements to the water system framework, further guaranteeing water security for the locale.

2. Balancing water supply and environmental impact

The administration of water assets is a squeezing worldwide test, and finding some kind of harmony between meeting water supply needs and limiting ecological effect is a complicated errand. As populaces develop and environmental change intensifies water shortage, taking into account the ecological outcomes of our actions is basic. In this paper, we will investigate the mind boggling nexus between water supply and natural effect, the difficulties it presents, and the methodologies for accomplishing a manageable harmony.

The Meaning of Adjusting Water Supply and Ecological Effect:

Water is fundamental for all types of life and is pivotal for different human exercises, including farming, industry, and homegrown use. Guaranteeing a sufficient and solid water supply is essential to human prosperity, monetary turn of events, and food security. In any case, the administration of water assets can have significant natural outcomes.

Adjusting water supply and ecological effect is crucial in light of multiple factors:

Natural Wellbeing: Sea-going biological systems, including streams, lakes, and wetlands, are unpredictably associated with earthly environments. Changes in water accessibility and quality can disturb these environments, prompting living space debasement and loss of biodiversity.

Water Quality: Contaminated water sources can hurt both the climate and human wellbeing. Adjusting water supply and ecological effect includes safeguarding water quality to guarantee safe drinking water and practical sea-going environments.

Biological system Administrations: Solid environments offer fundamental types of assistance, like water cleansing, flood guideline, and fertilization. Disturbing these administrations can have expansive ramifications for networks and economies.

Long haul Maintainability: Impractical water the executives practices can exhaust springs, prompting long haul water shortage. Adjusting water supply and natural effect is fundamental for guaranteeing water accessibility for people in the future.

Challenges in Adjusting Water Supply and Natural Effect:

Rivalry for Assets: Developing populaces and expanded requests for water assets for farming, industry, and homegrown use increase contest for restricted water supplies.

Environmental Change: Environmental change prompts adjusted precipitation designs, more incessant dry spells, and changing hydrological cycles. These progressions present difficulties for water asset the executives and compound water shortage.

Foundation Advancement: The development of dams, supplies, and water system frameworks can change stream and upset normal living spaces. These tasks are in many cases vital for water supply however can have negative natural effects.

Water Contamination: Modern release, horticultural overflow, and lacking wastewater treatment add to water contamination, hurting seagoing biological systems and human wellbeing.

Over-Extraction: Extreme groundwater siphoning can prompt spring consumption, land subsidence, and seawater interruption, adversely influencing both water supply and the climate.

Methodologies for Accomplishing an Equilibrium:

Coordinated Water Asset The board (IWRM): IWRM is a comprehensive methodology that thinks about the social, financial, and ecological elements of water asset the executives. It stresses partner investment and the practical utilization of water assets.

Environment Based Approaches: Integrating biological system based approaches into water the board includes considering the job of sound biological systems in keeping up with water quality and amount. This approach advances practical land use and natural surroundings protection.

Proficient Water Use: Advancing water-productive advancements, rural practices, and modern cycles can diminish water utilization and the natural effect of water use.

Water Reusing and Reuse: Treating and reusing wastewater for non-consumable purposes can lessen the interest on freshwater sources and relieve contamination.

Nature-Based Arrangements: Executing nature-based arrangements, like reforestation, wetland reclamation, and green framework, can further develop water quality, control stream, and upgrade strength to environmental change.

Environment Transformation: Creating environment tough water supply frameworks and practices can assist with alleviating the effects of environmental change on water accessibility and quality.

Administrative Systems: Compelling administrative structures are fundamental for overseeing water assets economically. These systems can lay out water freedoms, set water quality guidelines, and implement ecological assurances.

Contextual analyses in Adjusting Water Supply and Natural Effect:

Colorado Stream, USA: The Colorado Stream fills in as an essential water hotspot for a few US states and Mexico. Overallocation and drawn out dry spell have prompted critical ecological difficulties, including the drying of wetlands and declining fish populaces. Endeavors are in progress to reestablish the stream's wellbeing while at the same time meeting water supply needs through cooperative arrangements and water preservation measures.

Danube Stream, Europe: The Danube Waterway bowl traverses various European nations and countenances difficulties connected with contamination, living space corruption, and contending water utilizes. The European Association's Water System Mandate intends to accomplish a practical equilibrium by setting ecological goals and advancing transboundary collaboration.

Yellow Stream, China: The Yellow Stream is frequently alluded to as the "Distress of China" because of its continuous floods and low water levels. To adjust water supply and natural effect, China has executed different measures, including water redirection projects, wetland protection, and reforestation.

B. Construction and Challenges

Development is a foundation of human advancement, molding the world we occupy and giving the framework to present day cultures. From transcending high rises to unpredictable transportation organizations, development projects address accomplishments of designing and engineering. In any case, the business likewise wrestles with various provokes that reach from specialized intricacies to ecological worries. In this exposition, we will investigate the universe of development, its importance, the difficulties it faces, and creative ways to deal with beat them.

The Meaning of Development:

Framework Advancement: Development projects give the basic foundation expected to society to effectively work. This incorporates transportation organizations, energy frameworks, and utilities.

Monetary Development: The development business is a significant supporter of the economy, producing position and invigorating financial action. It is much of the time seen as an indicator of a country's financial wellbeing.

Personal satisfaction: Structures, homes, and public spaces made through development altogether influence individuals' personal satisfaction. Protected and agreeable designs work on prosperity.

Advancement and Plan: Development projects frequently push the limits of plan and designing, cultivating development in materials, procedures, and innovation.

Manageability: In a period of natural awareness, economical development rehearses are turning out to be progressively significant. Developing energy-effective, harmless to the ecosystem structures and framework mitigates environmental change.

Challenges in Development:

Cost Overwhelms: Development projects frequently surpass their underlying financial plans because of unexpected conditions, like changes in plan, weather conditions deferrals, or material expense variances.

Project Postponements: Deferrals can be brought about by various variables, including allowing issues, work deficiencies, and antagonistic weather patterns. These deferrals can be expensive and troublesome.

Quality Control: Guaranteeing that development fulfills quality guidelines is a diligent test. Surrenders and below average work can think twice about and strength.

Ecological Effect: Development exercises can have huge natural effects, including environment annihilation, contamination, and asset exhaustion. Feasible development rehearses are expected to alleviate these impacts.

Work Deficiencies: Gifted work deficiencies can prompt deferrals and expanded work costs. It is fundamental to Support preparing and labor force improvement.

Administrative Consistence: Exploring complex administrative systems and getting licenses can be tedious and exorbitant.

Wellbeing: Building locales can be hazardous, and guaranteeing the security of laborers is a first concern. Mishaps and wounds can prompt venture delays and inflated costs.

Creative Ways to deal with Beat Difficulties:

High level Undertaking The board: Utilizing progressed project the executives strategies, for example, Building Data Demonstrating (BIM) and Lean development, can improve productivity and lessen cost invades and delays.

Construction and Secluded Development: Pre-assembled parts and measured development strategies are acquiring prominence for their capability to accelerate development, lessen squander, and work on quality control.

Maintainability and Green Structure: Embracing green structure works on, including energy-effective plan and the utilization of supportable materials, can lessen natural effect and working expenses.

Mechanical Reconciliation: The mix of innovation, like robots, sensors, and mechanical technology, can further develop wellbeing, effectiveness, and information assortment on building locales.

Cooperative Venture Conveyance: Cooperative undertaking conveyance strategies, for example, plan fabricate and incorporated project conveyance (IPD), empower collaboration and hazard dividing between project partners, prompting improved results.

Computerized Twins: The idea of computerized twins includes making an advanced copy of a development project, considering continuous observing, investigation, and direction, which can assist with forestalling delays and further develop productivity.

Manageable Materials and Practices: The utilization of feasible structure materials, like reused and privately obtained materials, alongside rehearses like latent plan and water reaping, can lessen natural effect.

Contextual analyses in Imaginative Development:

The Burj Khalifa, Dubai: The Burj Khalifa, the world's tallest high rise, grandstands imaginative designing and development procedures, including a built up substantial construction, an elite presentation shade wall, and high level lifts.

The Masdar City, UAE: Masdar City in Abu Dhabi is a manageable metropolitan improvement project that focuses on energy productivity and sustainable power sources. It consolidates shrewd innovation, environmentally friendly power age, and green structure plans.

The Channel Passage, Europe: The Channel Passage, interfacing the Unified Realm and France, is a perfect representation of cooperative task conveyance. It included designing advancements, for example, burrow exhausting machines and security measures for submerged development.

1. Execution of the massive project

The effective execution of a gigantic undertaking is a demonstration of human resourcefulness, collaboration, and fastidious preparation. Whether it's the development of a megaproject like a high rise, the improvement of a state of the art mechanical development, or the acknowledgment of an aggressive framework drive, the method involved with transforming a terrific vision into an unmistakable the truth is a mind boggling venture. In this article, we will investigate the critical parts of executing gigantic activities, the difficulties in question, and the procedures for accomplishing fruitful results.

The Periods of Task Execution:

Project Commencement: This stage includes characterizing the task's targets, degree, financial plan, and timetable. It requires getting endorsements, getting financing, and collecting a venture group.

Nitty gritty Preparation: Point by point arranging is essential for outlining the venture's errands, courses of events, asset allotment, and chance administration systems. Project directors use instruments like Gantt graphs and basic way examination to plan and timetable exercises.

Asset Distribution: Apportioning assets, including HR, materials, gear, and innovation, is fundamental for guaranteeing that the venture advances without a hitch and effectively.

Execution: The execution stage includes completing the arranged exercises and assignments. It requires successful coordination, correspondence, and oversight to guarantee that work advances as per the arrangement.

Checking and Control: All through the task, observing and control systems are utilized to follow progress, distinguish deviations from the arrangement, and make restorative moves on a case by case basis.

Quality Confirmation: Guaranteeing the nature of work is a basic part of execution. Quality affirmation cycles, examinations, and testing are carried out to fulfill project guidelines.

Risk The board: Proactive gamble the executives is urgent to recognize expected chances and foster systems to moderate or address them during execution.

Partner Correspondence: Successful correspondence with partners, including project supports, colleagues, and outer gatherings, is fundamental for keep everybody educated and locked in.

Documentation and Detailing: Keeping exact records and reporting project progress, issues, and changes is fundamental for straightforwardness and responsibility.

Conclusion: The venture conclusion stage includes concluding movements of every sort, getting endorsements, directing task surveys, and progressing the undertaking expectations to the end-clients or proprietors.

Challenges in Executing Enormous Undertakings:

Intricacy: Enormous scope projects frequently include many-sided plans, various partners, and perplexing planned operations, making them intrinsically complicated.

Financial plan The executives: Dealing with the spending plan for huge ventures can be trying because of cost overwhelms, surprising costs, and changing monetary circumstances.

Asset Allotment: Designating and overseeing assets effectively can be troublesome, particularly in projects with high asset requests.

Scope Changes: Changes in project extension can disturb the execution cycle and lead to deferrals and spending plan increments.

Risk The board: Recognizing, evaluating, and alleviating chances is complicated in enormous undertakings because of their scale and degree.

Administrative Consistence: Following administrative necessities, ecological guidelines, and wellbeing guidelines can add layers of intricacy to project execution.

Combination of Innovation: Embracing and incorporating state of the art advancements into gigantic undertakings requires ability and can prompt unexpected difficulties.

Techniques for Effective Execution:

Hearty Undertaking The board: Viable task the executives is the foundation of fruitful execution. Talented undertaking administrators make definite plans, screen progress, and adjust to evolving conditions.

Clear Correspondence: Straightforward and continuous correspondence with all partners, including project groups, supports, and administrative bodies, is fundamental for progress.

Risk The board: Proactive gamble the executives implies recognizing potential dangers early, creating relief plans, and consistently checking and reevaluating gambles all through the venture.

Change The board: An organized way to deal with overseeing changes in project degree is basic to stay away from tasks running wild and keep up with project control.

Asset The executives: Proficient distribution and the board of assets, including gifted faculty and innovation, are crucial for convenient and savvy execution.

Quality Confirmation: Executing vigorous quality affirmation cycles and leading customary examinations and testing guarantee that work fulfills quality guidelines.

Execution Measurements: Laying out key execution pointers (KPIs) permits project chiefs to quantify headway and pursue information driven choices.

Contextual analyses in Fruitful Venture Execution:

The Panama Waterway Extension: The development of the Panama Channel, finished in 2016, involved the development of new locks to oblige bigger vessels. Regardless of mind boggling designing difficulties and monetary worries, the task was effectively executed, improving worldwide shipping lanes.

The Worldwide Space Station (ISS): The ISS, a cooperative exertion including different nations and associations, required exact preparation and execution. It remains as an image of world-wide collaboration and effective venture the board in space investigation.

The Fast Rail Organization in Japan: Japan's broad rapid rail organization, known as the Shinkansen, is an illustration of proficient execution and progressing advancement in transportation foundation.

2. **Overcoming hurdles and setbacks**

Life is loaded up with difficulties, obstructions, and mishaps that can appear to be unconquerable. Whether in private undertakings, proficient pursuits, or huge scope projects, misfortunes are an unavoidable piece of the excursion. In any case, it is in confronting these obstacles and beating them that people and associations can really flourish and accomplish their objectives. In this exposition, we will investigate the significance of flexibility, systems for defeating obstacles, and instances of people and gatherings who have transformed mishaps into venturing stones to progress.

The Meaning of Strength:

Mental Prosperity: Flexibility cultivates mental and close to home prosperity by assisting people with creating survival strategies to manage pressure and misfortune.

Proficient Achievement: In the work environment, versatility empowers representatives and pioneers to deal with misfortunes, adjust to evolving conditions, and stay useful and spurred.

Self-improvement: Defeating obstacles frequently prompts self-awareness and the securing of new abilities and points of view, at last upgrading one's capacities.

Critical thinking: Strength advances successful critical thinking abilities, empowering people to track down effective fixes to difficulties.

Long haul Achievement: Strength is a critical figure making long haul progress and maintainability, as it assists people and associations with persisting through troublesome times.

Techniques for Conquering Obstacles and Mishaps:

Keep a Development Mentality: Embrace difficulties as any open doors for development instead of as disappointments. A development mentality cultivates a conviction that capacities and knowledge can be created with exertion and learning.

Put forth Reasonable Objectives: Guarantee that your objectives are reachable and lined up with your capacities and assets. This lessens the probability of getting yourself positioned for pointless difficulties.

Look for Help: Feel free to out for help from companions, family, guides, or associates while confronting troubles. Sharing your difficulties can give significant bits of knowledge and basic encouragement.

Adjust and Be Adaptable: Be available to adjusting your methodologies and plans when conditions change. Adaptability is an essential resource while beating unforeseen obstacles.

Gain from Difficulties: Treat misfortunes as any open doors for learning. Break down what turned out badly, recognize regions for development, and apply those examples to future undertakings.

Remain Steady: Diligence despite difficulties is a sign of strength. Continue to pursue your objectives, in any event, when progress appears to be slow or obstructions seem overwhelming.

Keep a Positive Mentality: Develop an inspirational perspective by zeroing in on arrangements as opposed to harping on issues. Hopefulness can support your capacity to defeat obstacles.

Instances of Defeating Mishaps:

Thomas Edison and the Light: Thomas Edison, quite possibly of history's most productive designer, confronted various misfortunes while fostering the electric light. He broadly said, "I have not fizzled. I've recently found 10,000 different ways that won't work." Edison's tirelessness at last prompted the innovation of the commonsense glowing light.

J.K. Rowling and "Harry Potter": J.K. Rowling, the creator of the tremendously well known "Harry Potter" series, confronted various dismissals from distributers prior to making progress. Her assurance to see her vision through ultimately made her one of the most amazing selling creators on the planet.

NASA's Mars Meanderers: NASA's Mars wanderer missions, including Soul and Opportunity, confronted various difficulties, including specialized errors and correspondence issues. In spite of mishaps, the wanderers surpassed their normal life expectancies and made weighty disclosures on Mars.

Nelson Mandela's Detainment: Nelson Mandela, the counter politically-sanctioned racial segregation progressive and previous Leader of South Africa, got through 27

years of detainment for his activism. His strength, alongside the help of millions, prompted his possible delivery and the destroying of politically-sanctioned racial segregation.

SpaceX and Rocket Disappointments: SpaceX, drove by Elon Musk, encountered a few rocket disappointments in its initial years. In any case, the organization kept on refining its innovation and techniques, eventually accomplishing achievements like reusable rockets and manned spaceflight.

Chapter 4

Impact on Agriculture

Farming is the foundation of worldwide food security, giving food to billions of individuals and supporting economies around the world. In any case, agribusiness faces a variety of difficulties in the 21st 100 years, including environmental change, populace development, asset constraints, and moving buyer inclinations. This article will dive into the significant effect of these difficulties on horticulture, investigate imaginative transformations and arrangements, and examine what's to come possibilities of the rural area.

1. **The Ongoing Scene of Horticulture:**
   Significance of Agribusiness: Farming is the essential wellspring of food, fiber, and occupations for most of the total populace. It assumes a focal part in worldwide economies, country improvement, and food security.
   Worldwide Food Interest: The worldwide populace is projected to reach 9.7 billion by 2050. This significant populace development will fundamentally expand the interest for food and agrarian items.
   Environmental Change: Environmental change presents one of

the most squeezing dangers to agribusiness. It prompts expanded temperatures, modified precipitation examples, and more incessant outrageous climate occasions, all of which can upset crop creation and effect food security.

Asset Shortage: Restricted admittance to freshwater, arable land, and other fundamental assets presents difficulties to agribusiness. Abuse of water assets, soil debasement, and deforestation further strain the area.

Financial and Market Influences: The farming business is impacted by monetary elements, including product costs, exchange arrangements, and market instability. These variables can influence the productivity and supportability of cultivating rehearses.

Mechanical Progressions: Headways in innovation, like accuracy farming, hereditarily changed yields, and mechanization, are reshaping the horticultural scene by expanding efficiency and effectiveness.

2. **Effect of Environmental Change on Farming:**

    Adjusted Developing Seasons: Changing temperatures and modified precipitation examples can upset conventional developing seasons, influencing crop yields and establishing windows.

    Outrageous Climate Occasions: Expanded recurrence and seriousness of outrageous climate occasions, like dry seasons, floods, and heatwaves, can harm harvests, domesticated animals, and foundation.

    Bug and Illness Episodes: Environmental change can make positive circumstances for vermin and sicknesses, influencing both yield and animals creation.

    Water Shortage: Lessening freshwater assets and changing precipitation examples can prompt water shortage, influencing water system and animals the board.

    Loss of Biodiversity: Environmental change can modify biological systems and disturb the fragile equilibrium between vegetation that help horticulture, influencing fertilization and normal vermin control.

3. **Versatile Procedures in Farming:**

   Environment Versatile Yield Assortments: Creating and taking on crop assortments that are more impervious to intensity, dry season, and bugs can improve strength to environmental change.

   Feasible Cultivating Practices: Practices like protection horticulture, crop revolution, and natural cultivating advance soil wellbeing and lessen ecological effects.

   Further developed Water The executives: Carrying out proficient water system frameworks, water collecting, and water-saving advancements can assist with overseeing water shortage.

   Environment Data and Estimating: Admittance to precise environment data and determining can assist ranchers with arriving at informed conclusions about planting and collecting times.

   Agroforestry and Biodiversity Protection: Coordinating trees and various plant species into cultivating frameworks can upgrade soil richness, give shade, and backing biodiversity.

   Environment Savvy Domesticated animals Cultivating: Executing environment versatile domesticated animals the executives rehearses, for example, worked on reproducing and sustenance, guarantees food security.

4. **Mechanical Headways in Agribusiness:**

   Accuracy Horticulture: Using information driven innovations, sensors, and GPS frameworks to streamline ranch the executives, diminish asset use, and increment efficiency.

   Hereditarily Changed Yields: The improvement of hereditarily adjusted organic entities (GMOs) can upgrade crop protection from nuisances, sicknesses, and natural stressors.

   Vertical Cultivating and Controlled Climate Agribusiness: These imaginative methodologies consider all year crop creation in metropolitan settings, lessening the requirement for customary farmland.

Mechanization and Advanced mechanics: Computerization innovation, like robots and independent work vehicles, can perform assignments like planting, collecting, and checking, expanding productivity and decreasing work necessities.

Blockchain and Detectability: Blockchain innovation is being utilized to further develop inventory network straightforwardness and recognizability, guaranteeing the security and validness of food items.

5. **The Job of Strategy and Administration:**

Government Strategies: States assume a significant part in molding horticultural practices and maintainability through strategies connected with sponsorships, land use, exchange, and natural guidelines.

Worldwide Collaboration: Worldwide associations and arrangements, like the Unified Countries' Supportable Advancement Objectives and the Paris Understanding, advance global participation and manageable horticultural practices.

Ranchers' Freedoms: Enabling limited scope ranchers and guaranteeing their privileges to land, assets, and fair business sectors are fundamental for feasible horticulture.

Exploration and Expansion Administrations: Putting resources into agrarian examination, instruction, and augmentation administrations can furnish ranchers with the information and apparatuses expected to embrace supportable practices.

6. **Future Possibilities for Farming:**

Reasonable Heightening: Offsetting expanded food creation with natural maintainability will be an essential concentration. Practical heightening expects to deliver more food with less assets.

Metropolitan Horticulture: As urbanization proceeds, metropolitan farming and vertical cultivating will assume a critical part in satisfying neighborhood food need.

Computerized Farming: The coordination of innovation, information examination, and man-made consciousness will keep on changing agribusiness by further developing independent direction and asset the executives.

Roundabout Agribusiness: Embracing roundabout economy standards, where waste is limited, and assets are reused or reused, will decrease the ecological impression of farming.

Shopper Inclinations: Moving buyer inclinations toward supportable, privately obtained, and natural food varieties will impact creation practices and supply chains.

1. Agricultural Transformation

Farming has been a basic piece of human development for centuries, giving food, livelihoods, and social characters. Be that as it may, in the 21st 100 years, farming countenances a squeezing need for change to address different difficulties, including worldwide populace development, environmental change, asset shortage, and advancing buyer inclinations. This paper investigates the idea of horticultural change, its importance, key drivers, and the way toward feasible food frameworks.

1. **Grasping Agrarian Change:**
   Farming change alludes to a significant and foundational shift in the manner rural practices are directed, portrayed by tremendous changes in innovation, strategies, establishments, and the association of horticultural frameworks. Such changes are
   driven by different factors and intend to improve food security, ecological supportability, and financial turn of events.
2. **Meaning of Agrarian Change:**
   Food Security: With the worldwide populace expected to arrive at 9.7 billion by 2050, agrarian change is urgent for fulfilling the rising need for food.
   Ecological Maintainability: Customary cultivating rehearses

have frequently prompted natural corruption, including deforestation, soil disintegration, and water contamination. Changing horticulture is fundamental to alleviate these effects.

Financial Turn of events: Farming is a significant supporter of the economies of numerous nations, particularly those in the creating scene. Rural change can spike monetary development, lessen neediness, and set out work open doors.

Environmental Change Relief: Farming is both helpless against and a supporter of environmental change. Changing horticulture to be more environment versatile and less outflows escalated is basic for relieving environmental change.

Nourishing Quality: Rural change can likewise work on the wholesome nature of food, tending to hunger and eat less carbs related medical problems.

3. **Key Drivers of Rural Change:**

Mechanical Progressions: The reception of cutting edge rural innovations, like accuracy horticulture, biotechnology, and advanced cultivating, can fundamentally increment efficiency and lessen asset use.

Strategy Changes: Legislatures assume a crucial part in horticultural change through arrangement mediations that advance feasible practices, further develop market access, and give motivators to advancement.

Institutional Changes: Reinforcing agrarian establishments, including research associations, augmentation administrations, and rancher cooperatives, can improve the limit of ranchers to take on present day rehearses.

Market Access: Further developing admittance to business sectors, both homegrown and global, can furnish ranchers with better costs and impetuses for taking on supportable practices.

Environment Strong Agribusiness: The improvement of environment versatile yield assortments and animals breeds is critical for adjusting to changing environment conditions.

4. **Pathways to Supportable Rural Change:**

   Expansion: Empowering crop enhancement can further develop flexibility to vermin, sicknesses, and environment fluctuation. It can likewise improve the dietary nature of diets by advancing the development of various yields.

   Protection Horticulture: Practices like least culturing, crop pivot, and cover editing can lessen soil disintegration, further develop soil wellbeing, and improve long haul supportability.

   Manageable Strengthening: Offsetting expanded food creation with natural manageability includes embracing rehearses that boost yields while limiting asset use and ecological effects.

   Advanced Agribusiness: The joining of computerized innovations, information investigation, and man-made consciousness can further develop direction, asset the executives, and market access for ranchers.

   Round Economy Standards: Carrying out roundabout economy standards, where waste is limited, and assets are reused or reused, can diminish the ecological impression of horticulture.

5. **Contextual analyses in Farming Change:**

   The Green Transformation: The Green Upheaval of the mid-twentieth century achieved sensational expansions in crop yields through the presentation of high-yielding harvest assortments, further developed water system, and manufactured composts. Notwithstanding, it additionally raised worries about ecological supportability and value.

   Accuracy Agribusiness in the US: Accuracy horticulture works on, including GPS-directed farm vehicles and robots for crop checking, have altered cultivating in the US. These innovations have improved efficiency and asset proficiency.

   Economical Cultivating in the Netherlands: The Netherlands has embraced supportable horticulture rehearses, for example, accuracy cultivating, coordinated bug the board, and maintainable animals cultivating. These drives have diminished natural effects while keeping up with high agrarian efficiency.

Natural Cultivating in India: India has seen huge development in natural cultivating, driven by shopper interest for better and harmless to the ecosystem items. Natural cultivating rehearses focus on soil wellbeing, biodiversity, and decreased synthetic use.

6. **Difficulties and Contemplations:**

Disparity: Rural change should consider issues of value, guaranteeing that limited scale ranchers and underestimated networks benefit from these changes.

Asset Shortage: Tending to asset restrictions, including freshwater accessibility and arable land, is pivotal for economical agrarian change.

Environmental Change: Environment tough practices and variation systems are fundamental for horticulture's drawn out supportability in an evolving environment.

Buyer Conduct: Moving customer inclinations toward maintainable, privately obtained, and natural food varieties can impact creation practices and supply chains.

1. Improved irrigation and crop patterns

Farming is the foundation of food creation, and its manageability is urgent for worldwide food security. In any case, farming countenances various difficulties, including changing environment designs, water shortage, and soil debasement. Further developed water system and yield designs are fundamental parts of current horticultural practices pointed toward tending to these difficulties, upgrading crop efficiency, and guaranteeing long haul manageability. In this paper, we will dig into the meaning of further developed water system strategies and improved crop designs, their effect on farming, and the way to accomplishing a more reasonable food future.

1. **Meaning of Further developed Water system:**
   Upgraded Water The executives: Further developed water system strategies empower more proficient water use, limiting wastage and diminishing the burden on water assets.
   Moderation of Dry season: In districts inclined to dry season, high level water system techniques can give a life saver to ranchers, assisting them with keeping up with crop yields during droughts.
   Further developed Harvest Yields: Legitimate water system guarantees that yields get the important measure of dampness, prompting expanded yields and food creation.
   Supportability: Maintainable water system practices can assist with forestalling soil disintegration and salinization, saving the drawn out efficiency of horticultural land.

2. **High level Water system Procedures:**
   Dribble Water system: Trickle water system conveys water straightforwardly to the root zone of plants through an organization of lines and tubing. This strategy limits water wastage and is exceptionally productive.
   Sprinkler Water system: Sprinkler frameworks disperse water over crops as beads, like regular precipitation. They are reasonable for different harvests and can decrease water utilization contrasted with conventional strategies.
   Subsurface Dribble Water system (SDI): SDI places water system lines beneath the dirt surface, diminishing water dissipation and limiting weed development.
   Accuracy Water system: Accuracy water system joins innovation, information investigation, and mechanized frameworks to convey exact measures of water to crops in view of their particular necessities, improving water use productivity.

3. **Influence on Yield Examples:**
   Crop Turn: Substituting the sorts of harvests developed on a specific land parcel can assist with forestalling soil consumption, decrease bug and infection pressure, and further develop soil

wellbeing.

Crop Broadening: Growing different harvests on a solitary ranch can upgrade flexibility to unfavorable weather patterns, vermin, and market changes.

Intercropping: Intercropping includes establishing various harvests in nearness. It can upgrade supplement cycling, decrease soil disintegration, and further develop generally yield dependability.

Cover Yields: Cover crops are established between principal crop seasons to safeguard soil from disintegration, fix nitrogen, and further develop soil structure.

4. **Feasible Agribusiness and Protection:**

Protection Culturing: Decreasing or wiping out culturing can assist with rationing soil dampness, diminish disintegration, and sequester carbon in the dirt.

Agroforestry: Joining trees or bushes with yields or animals on a similar land parcel can give conceal, further develop soil ripeness, and backing biodiversity.

Natural Cultivating: Natural cultivating rehearses focus on soil wellbeing, keeping away from manufactured synthetic compounds and zeroing in on normal techniques for bother control and supplement the executives.

Coordinated Nuisance The executives (IPM): IPM joins natural, physical, and compound methodologies to oversee bugs while limiting damage to the climate.

5. **Difficulties and Contemplations:**

Mechanical and Monetary Hindrances: Admittance to cutting edge water system innovation and feasible cultivating practices can be restricted, particularly for limited scope ranchers in creating districts.

Conduct Change: Executing further developed water system and harvest designs frequently expects ranchers to change their customary practices, which can be trying without instruction and backing.

Water Freedoms and Access: Powerful water system frequently relies upon secure water privileges and admittance to water sources, which can be perplexing and antagonistic in certain districts.

6. **Contextual analyses:**

Israel's Trickle Water system Achievement: Israel is a trailblazer in dribble water system innovation, permitting it to boost crop creation in a water-scant locale. This innovation has been taken on worldwide, further developing water use effectiveness.

Crop Pivot in the Midwest, USA: In the American Midwest, ranchers practice crop revolution, including the development of maize, soybeans, and wheat. This training keeps up with soil fruitfulness and decreases the gamble of irritation pervasions.

7. **The Way to an Economical Food Future:**

Instruction and Preparing: Giving ranchers information and preparing on cutting edge water system strategies and economical cultivating rehearses is urgent for reception.

Monetary Help: States and associations can offer monetary motivating forces, endowments, and admittance to reasonable credit to assist ranchers with putting resources into further developed water system frameworks and manageable practices.

Exploration and Advancement: Progressing examination and advancement are imperative to growing new and more effective water system strategies, as well as distinguishing the most reasonable harvest designs for various districts.

Strategy Structures: Legislatures ought to execute arrangements that empower reasonable horticulture, remembering guidelines for water use, motivators for protection practices, and backing for innovative work.

2. Increased agricultural productivity

Farming efficiency is a foundation of worldwide food security and financial soundness. With the total populace projected to surpass 9 billion by 2050, the interest for food will keep on rising. Expanding horticultural efficiency has turned into a basic to guarantee a consistent food supply while limiting the natural effect of cultivating. In this paper, we will investigate the meaning of expanded farming efficiency, the different variables that impact it, and the systems utilized to economically upgrade efficiency.

1. **Meaning of Expanded Horticultural Efficiency:**
   Food Security: Upgraded horticultural efficiency is fundamental for fulfill the rising worldwide need for food. A strong food supply forestalls yearning and unhealthiness, especially in creating districts.

   Monetary Development: Farming is a huge supporter of the economies of numerous nations. Expanded efficiency can support farming pay, make occupations, and invigorate financial development.

   Asset Proficiency: By creating more food on existing rural land, efficiency gains diminish the need to grow horticultural wildernesses, assisting with saving regular environments and biodiversity.

   Environment Flexibility: Efficiency enhancements can make farming stronger with the impacts of environmental change, guaranteeing that food creation stays stable notwithstanding outrageous climate occasions and moving climatic circumstances.

2. **Factors Affecting Agrarian Efficiency:**
   Innovative Progressions: The turn of events and reception of cutting edge agrarian advancements, like hereditarily altered crops, accuracy agribusiness, and computerized hardware, have essentially expanded efficiency.

   Crop The board: Further developed crop the executives works on, including crop pivot, supplement the board, and irritation control, can improve yields and diminish misfortunes.

   Water system: Legitimate water system strategies guarantee that yields get the important water, particularly in areas with sporadic precipitation designs.

Plant Rearing: The improvement of high-yielding harvest assortments that are impervious to vermin and illnesses plays had a urgent impact in helping efficiency.

Admittance to Information sources: Ranchers' admittance to quality seeds, manures, and pesticides fundamentally impacts their capacity to increment crop yields.

3. **Systems for Improving Rural Efficiency:**

   Supportable Strengthening: Maintainable increase tries to amplify rural creation while limiting negative natural effects. It includes practices, for example, accuracy cultivating, incorporated bug the board, and soil protection.

   Crop Expansion: Growing various yields can assist with lessening the gamble of harvest disappointment because of nuisance invasions or unfriendly atmospheric conditions.

   Schooling and Expansion Administrations: Giving ranchers preparing and data on best farming practices is fundamental for further developing efficiency.

   Innovative work: Putting resources into farming exploration, especially on crop reproducing and new advancements, can prompt forward leaps that increment efficiency.

   Market Access: Further developing admittance to business sectors permits ranchers to sell their items at better costs, giving an impetus to expanded creation.

4. **Feasible Horticulture and Efficiency:**

   Natural Cultivating: Natural cultivating rehearses center around supportability by staying away from engineered synthetics and focusing on normal irritation control and soil wellbeing.

   Agroecology: Agroecological approaches incorporate biological standards into horticultural frameworks to advance maintainability, strength, and efficiency.

   Protection Agribusiness: Preservation farming limits soil unsettling influence, keeps up with soil cover, and elevates crop pivot to work on long haul efficiency.

5. **Contextual analyses in Expanded Rural Efficiency:**
The Green Upheaval: The Green Unrest of the mid-twentieth century saw critical expansions in rural efficiency through the presentation of high-yielding harvest assortments, current water system strategies, and engineered manures. It assumed a crucial part in tending to food shortage in a few districts.

China's Agrarian Change: China's rural change in ongoing many years has been set apart by expanded efficiency through the reception of current cultivating rehearses, mechanical progressions, and further developed admittance to business sectors.

6. **Difficulties and Contemplations:**

Ecological Effect: Expanding efficiency frequently accompanies natural expenses, like expanded water utilization, pesticide spillover, and soil corruption. Offsetting efficiency with maintainability is a test.

Asset Shortage: Admittance to fundamental assets like water and arable land can restrict efficiency upgrades, particularly in areas confronting asset imperatives.

Market Access: Inconsistent market access can keep limited scope ranchers from profiting from expanded efficiency, as they might confront difficulties in selling their excess produce.

B. Socio-economic Upliftment

Financial upliftment, otherwise called financial turn of events, alludes to the most common way of further developing the monetary and social prosperity of people and networks. It includes many drives and strategies pointed toward diminishing neediness, advancing value, and upgrading the personal satisfaction for all citizenry. In this paper, we will investigate the meaning of financial upliftment, its key parts, and the methodologies utilized to accomplish it.

1. **The Meaning of Financial Upliftment:**
   Lessening Destitution: Financial upliftment is a pivotal device for neediness lightening. By working on the monetary states of burdened populaces, it assists lift with peopling out of neediness.
   Advancing Value: It plans to decrease pay and abundance abberations, guaranteeing that potential open doors and advantages are all the more equally disseminated among all citizenry.
   Upgrading Personal satisfaction: Financial advancement tries to work on the general personal satisfaction by resolving issues like admittance to training, medical services, clean water, and disinfection.
   Animating Monetary Development: By putting resources into human resources and framework, financial upliftment can add to financial development and success.
   Cultivating Social Attachment: It helps assemble additional comprehensive social orders where people from assorted foundations can partake completely and calmly in their networks.

2. **Key Parts of Financial Upliftment:**
   Training: Admittance to quality instruction is major to financial turn of events. It enables people with information and abilities, improving their employability and pay acquiring potential.
   Medical services: Satisfactory medical services administrations, including preventive consideration and therapy, are fundamental for a sound and useful populace.
   Monetary Open doors: Making position, supporting business venture, and advancing feasible jobs are key to financial upliftment.
   Foundation Advancement: Interests in framework, like transportation, energy, and disinfection, are basic for monetary development and worked on everyday environments.
   Social Security Nets: Social wellbeing nets, including government assistance projects and joblessness benefits, give a security net to weak populaces during critical crossroads.

Orientation Correspondence: Advancing orientation balance by guaranteeing equivalent open doors and privileges for all sexes is a critical part of financial turn of events.

3. **Systems for Accomplishing Financial Upliftment:**

Schooling Access: Growing admittance to quality instruction, particularly for minimized gatherings, is critical. This remembers ventures for schools, grants, and grown-up training programs.

Medical care Access: Further developing admittance to medical care administrations, especially in underserved regions, can be accomplished through the development of medical services offices, preparing of medical services laborers, and sponsoring medical services costs for poor people.

Destitution Mitigation Projects: Executing designated neediness lightening programs, for example, cash moves, microcredit plans, and professional preparation, can give quick alleviation and backing independence.

Foundation Speculation: Framework advancement, including streets, spans, energy networks, and sterilization offices, can animate financial development and work on expectations for everyday comforts.

Business Age: Advancing position creation through open and confidential area speculations, work market arrangements, and abilities improvement projects can lessen joblessness and underemployment.

Comprehensive Monetary Arrangements: Guaranteeing that financial strategies are comprehensive and don't excessively help explicit gatherings is fundamental for impartial financial turn of events.

4. **Contextual analyses in Financial Upliftment:**

South Korea's Financial Supernatural occurrence: South Korea's fast industrialization and monetary development, known as the "Marvel on the Han Waterway," lifted the country from present conflict neediness on a flourishing, top level salary country.

Key elements remembered a concentration for instruction, trade drove development, and designated government strategies.

Brazil's Bolsa Família: The Bolsa Família program in Brazil gives cash moves to unfortunate families, dependent upon their youngsters going to class and getting medical care check-ups. This program has decreased neediness and work on friendly markers.

5. Difficulties and Contemplations:

Disparity: Tending to pay and abundance imbalance stays a huge test in numerous social orders. Financial upliftment should make progress toward additional impartial results.

Admittance to Assets: Guaranteeing that underestimated and weak populaces approach assets, valuable open doors, and social administrations is basic.

Manageability: Financial improvement ought to be sought after in a practical way that doesn't drain normal assets or mischief the climate.

1. Changes in livelihoods and rural communities

Provincial people group have for quite some time been the foundation of agrarian and customary occupations, molding the social, social, and monetary texture of countries all over the planet. Nonetheless, these networks are going through huge changes driven by globalization, innovative progressions, ecological changes, and moving socioeconomics. This exposition will investigate the progressions in livelihoods inside provincial networks, the difficulties they face, and the open doors for transformation and feasible turn of events.

1. Changing Jobs in Rustic People group:

Rural Change: Conventional means cultivating is developing into more business and innovatively progressed agribusiness. Present day cultivating procedures, including accuracy horticulture and hereditarily adjusted crops, are changing the idea of country work.

Movement: Rustic to-metropolitan relocation is a huge pattern, as more youthful ages look for better monetary open doors and personal satisfaction in metropolitan regions. This shift has segment suggestions for rustic networks.

Broadening: Numerous country families are expanding their pay sources by participating in non-ranch exercises like rustic the travel industry, painstaking work, and private ventures. This diminishes monetary weakness.

Innovation Reception: Admittance to data and correspondence advances is working on in rustic regions, considering web based business, online schooling, and computerized business venture.

Ecological Changes: Environmental change and natural corruption can upset conventional occupations through adjusted atmospheric conditions, expanded nuisances, and soil debasement.

2. **Challenges Looked by Rustic People group:**

Monetary Abberations: Provincial people group frequently face higher neediness rates and lower wages contrasted with metropolitan regions, prompting financial variations.

Restricted Admittance to Administrations: Country regions might need admittance to fundamental administrations like medical services, instruction, and transportation, influencing the personal satisfaction and human resources advancement.

Horticultural Difficulties: Environment inconstancy, land corruption, and absence of admittance to current cultivating advancements can block farming efficiency.

Youth Movement: The outmigration of youth to metropolitan regions can bring about a maturing rustic populace, with suggestions for the progression of conventional jobs and local area attachment.

Social Confinement: Country people group might encounter social segregation because of restricted social cooperations, restricted admittance to social conveniences, and inadequate network.

3. **Potential open doors for Variation and Economical Turn of events:**

   Feasible Horticulture: Advancing economical cultivating rehearses, like natural cultivating, agroforestry, and preservation farming, can improve provincial jobs while safeguarding the climate.

   Esteem Option: Enhancing horticultural items through handling, marking, and showcasing can increment provincial livelihoods and set out work open doors.

   Computerized Network: Growing admittance to the web and advanced advances can work with web based business, online training, and remote work in provincial regions.

   Country The travel industry: Utilizing the regular magnificence, culture, and legacy of rustic regions can draw in vacationers, producing pay for neighborhood networks.

   Schooling and Abilities Improvement: Putting resources into instruction and expertise advancement projects can engage provincial inhabitants with the information and abilities required for different job choices.

4. **Contextual analyses in Country Business Changes:**

   Country Change in China: China's rustic regions have seen huge changes as millions have moved to urban areas for work. The public authority has answered with strategies to advance country business venture, modernize horticulture, and further develop framework.

   Agri-the travel industry in Italy: Italy has effectively evolved agri-the travel industry, where guests experience country life, take part in cultivating exercises, and appreciate neighborhood food. This has renewed numerous provincial networks.

5. **Government Approaches and Backing:**

   Country Improvement Projects: States can carry out provincial advancement programs that emphasis on foundation advancement, admittance to medical services and schooling, and occupation creation.

Rural Strategies: Arrangements that help economical cultivating rehearses, give admittance to credit, and guarantee fair evaluating for horticultural items are fundamental.

Advanced Consideration: Extending broadband web access and computerized education projects can connect the computerized split among provincial and metropolitan regions.

Land Change: Land residency security and evenhanded land conveyance can work on the livelihoods of rustic ranchers and advance rural turn of events.

6. **Challenges in Variation:**

Admittance to Assets: Restricted admittance to assets, including area and credit, can impede provincial networks' capacity to adjust and expand their jobs.

Strategy Execution: Powerful execution of country advancement approaches can be trying because of managerial issues, defilement, and deficient subsidizing.

Environmental Change: Adjusting to the effects of environmental change, like dry spells and outrageous climate occasions, can be exorbitant and require specialized mastery.

2. Alleviating poverty through water access

Admittance to spotless and dependable water is a central basic freedom and a basic consider the battle against neediness. For the overwhelming majority ruined networks all over the planet, the absence of satisfactory water access propagates a pattern of difficulty, influencing wellbeing, schooling, monetary open doors, and generally personal satisfaction. In this article, we will dive into the meaning of reducing destitution through superior water access, the difficulties looked in accomplishing this objective, and the methodologies utilized to achieve positive change.

1. **The Meaning of Water Access in Lightening Neediness:**
   Wellbeing and Prosperity: Safe drinking water and appropriate sterilization are fundamental for forestalling waterborne illnesses. Further developed water access can essentially diminish ailment and death rates, especially among youngsters.

   Schooling: When individuals, particularly kids, need to go through hours every day bringing water, it can restrict their admittance to instruction. Further developed water access saves time for schooling, further developing proficiency rates and future financial possibilities.

   Monetary Efficiency: Admittance to water for water system and domesticated animals prompts expanded horticultural efficiency, supporting food security and pay for provincial networks. Furthermore, admittance to water can uphold microenterprises and private companies.

   Orientation Strengthening: In numerous social orders, ladies and young ladies are principally answerable for water assortment. Further developed water access can lessen the weight on them, permitting them to take part in pay creating exercises and schooling.

   Ecological Supportability: Feasible water the executives practices can assist with preserving normal assets, safeguard biological systems, and guarantee long haul admittance to clean water for people in the future.

2. **Challenges in Lightening Neediness through Water Access:**
   Foundation Shortages: Many ruined regions need legitimate framework for water supply and sterilization, making it trying to give solid access.

   Water Shortage: In certain districts, water shortage is a huge test because of dry spells, over-extraction of groundwater, and environmental change influences.

   Defilement: Polluted water sources represent an extreme wellbeing risk. Waterborne illnesses, frequently brought about by insufficient disinfection, can subvert endeavors to further develop water access.

Monetary Obstructions: Low-pay networks might battle to bear the cost of the forthright expenses of building and keeping up with water foundation.

3. **Methodologies for Reducing Neediness through Water Access:**

   Interest in Foundation: Legislatures, NGOs, and worldwide associations can put resources into building and keeping up with water supply frameworks, for example, boreholes, wells, and funneled water organizations.

   Local area Based Approaches: Connecting with networks in the preparation, development, and the executives of water frameworks encourages a feeling of pride and maintainability.

   Water Reaping: Water gathering frameworks can give a decentralized and financially savvy wellspring of clean water, especially in dry locales.

   WASH Projects: Water, Sterilization, and Cleanliness (WASH) programs advance great cleanliness practices and disinfection close by water admittance to augment medical advantages.

   Water Estimating Approaches: Executing fair valuing strategies can assist with guaranteeing that water stays reasonable for low-pay families while taking care of the expenses of framework support.

4. **Contextual analyses in Reducing Neediness through Water Access:**

   Bangladesh's Protected Water Program: Bangladesh has taken critical steps in further developing water access through local area cooperation and the establishment of millions of hand-siphon tube wells. This drive has diminished waterborne illnesses and worked on generally speaking prosperity.

   The Water and Disinfection Program in Ghana: Ghana's program has centered around building sterilization and water supply offices in country regions. It has brought about better wellbeing, monetary open doors, and orientation strengthening.

5. Challenges in Execution:

Subsidizing Requirements: Satisfactory financing for water framework and support can be quite difficult for some legislatures and associations.

Limit Building: Nearby limit with regards to overseeing and keeping up with water frameworks might should be created to guarantee manageability.

Social and Social Factors: A few networks might oppose changes in water the board rehearses because of social standards or social progressive systems.

Chapter 5

Environmental Considerations

Natural contemplations are at the very front of worldwide conversations in the 21st hundred years. As the world wrestles with difficulties, for example, environmental change, biodiversity misfortune, contamination, and asset exhaustion, the requirement for mindful and maintainable natural practices has never been more dire. This far reaching article will dig into different parts of natural contemplations, including their importance, central questions, arrangements, and the job of people, associations, and legislatures in tending to them.

1. **The Meaning of Ecological Contemplations:**
   Planetary Wellbeing: Ecological wellbeing is unpredictably connected to human wellbeing. The prosperity of the planet straightforwardly influences the personal satisfaction for every single living creature, including people.

   Monetary Ramifications: Natural debasement can prompt financial misfortunes because of the expense of tending to ecological emergencies, decreased rural efficiency, and harm to foundation.

   Asset Shortage: As worldwide populaces keep on developing, the maintainable administration of normal assets, including water, energy, and arable land, becomes basic to stay away from asset shortage.

Environmental Change: The outcomes of environmental change, for example, rising ocean levels, outrageous climate occasions, and interruptions to biological systems, highlight the requirement for ecological contemplations.

2. **Key Ecological Issues:**

Environmental Change: The consuming of non-renewable energy sources, deforestation, and modern cycles discharge ozone depleting substances, prompting an Earth-wide temperature boost and environmental change influences like more successive and serious climate occasions.

Biodiversity Misfortune: Living space annihilation, poaching, contamination, and obtrusive species undermine biodiversity, prompting the eradication of many plant and creature species.

Contamination: Air, water, and soil contamination present huge wellbeing gambles and ecological difficulties, influencing biological systems, human wellbeing, and natural life.

Asset Exhaustion: Overexploitation of regular assets, like freshwater, woods, and fisheries, is prompting asset consumption and imperiling the accessibility of these assets for people in the future.

Squander The executives: The ill-advised removal of waste, remembering plastic contamination for seas and landfills, has extreme ecological outcomes.

3. **Arrangements and Systems:**

Environmentally friendly power Progress: Changing to environmentally friendly power sources like sun based, wind, and hydroelectric power can lessen ozone harming substance outflows and battle environmental change.

Supportable Horticulture: Taking on maintainable rural practices, like natural cultivating, crop revolution, and agroforestry, can advance food security and decrease the ecological effect of cultivating.

Preservation: Safeguarding and reestablishing regular living spaces through protection endeavors and reforestation can assist with saving biodiversity.

Roundabout Economy: Embracing a round economy model, where assets are reused, reused, and squander is limited, can lessen asset consumption and waste age.

Green Innovation: Creating and embracing green advancements, including energy-proficient apparatuses and electric vehicles, can lessen natural effects.

4. **Job of People:**

Maintainable Way of life Decisions: People can diminish their carbon impression by going with supportable decisions, for example, monitoring energy, decreasing waste, and picking eco-accommodating items.

Shopper Activism: Supporting organizations that focus on maintainability and capable ecological practices through buying choices can drive change on the lookout.

Ecological Backing: People can bring issues to light about natural issues and backer for strategy changes at the neighborhood, public, and global levels.

5. **Job of Associations:**

Corporate Obligation: Organizations can take on naturally capable works on, including decreasing emanations, executing feasible stock chains, and limiting waste.

Exploration and Advancement: Exploration establishments and organizations can put resources into advancement to foster harmless to the ecosystem innovations and arrangements.

Natural Certificate: Associations can look for and advance confirmations, like LEED (Administration in Energy and Ecological Plan), to show their obligation to supportability.

6. **Job of State run administrations:**

Strategy and Guideline: State run administrations can establish and implement ecological guidelines to restrict contamination, safeguard regular assets, and advance feasible practices.

Motivators and Appropriations: Legislatures can give impetuses and endowments to environmentally friendly power, green foundation, and reasonable cultivating rehearses.

Worldwide Participation: Cooperative endeavors among countries are fundamental for address worldwide ecological difficulties, for example, environmental change and biodiversity misfortune.

7. **Contextual analyses in Natural Contemplations:**

Sustainable power in Germany: Germany's Energiewende (energy change) strategy has prompted huge expansions in sustainable power creation, diminishing ozone harming substance discharges and dependence on petroleum derivatives.

Preservation in Costa Rica: Costa Rica's broad protection endeavors and installment for environment administrations programs have safeguarded a significant piece of its biodiversity and drawn in ecotourism income.

8. **Difficulties and Contemplations:**

Monetary Interests: Offsetting natural contemplations with financial interests can challenge, as certain strategies and practices might influence enterprises and occupations.

Worldwide Disparity: The weight of natural difficulties frequently falls excessively on weak populaces, requiring evenhanded arrangements.

Political Will: The political will to institute and uphold ecological approaches can be affected by different elements, including campaigning by strong enterprises.

1. **Ecological Impact**

The biological effect of human exercises on the climate has become progressively obvious in late many years. As the worldwide populace develops and industrialization proceeds, the regular world faces a large number of dangers, from living space obliteration to contamination to environmental change. In this article, we will investigate the meaning of biological effect, analyze major questions, and examine answers for moderate the unfortunate results of human activities on the climate.

1. **The Meaning of Natural Effect:**

   Biodiversity Misfortune: Human exercises like deforestation, living space obliteration, and over-abuse of assets are driving species termination rates to remarkable levels. Biodiversity misfortune compromises the steadiness of environments and decreases the flexibility of the planet.

   Environmental Change: The consuming of non-renewable energy sources, deforestation, and modern cycles discharge ozone depleting substances, prompting a worldwide temperature alteration and changes in environment designs. These progressions have extensive biological outcomes, influencing everything from polar ice covers to coral reefs.

   Contamination: Contamination of air, water, and soil unfavorably affects environments and human wellbeing. Synthetic toxins, plastics, and weighty metals can disturb normal cycles and mischief natural life.

   Land Use Change: Urbanization, agribusiness, and framework advancement frequently bring about land use changes that section living spaces, prompting the confinement of species populaces and diminished hereditary variety.

2. **Key Biological Issues:**

   Living space Annihilation: The transformation of normal environments into metropolitan regions, farming, and foundation improvement brings about natural surroundings misfortune and discontinuity, affecting endless species and biological systems.

   Over-double-dealing: Over-collecting of regular assets, for example, overfishing and unlawful untamed life exchange, drains populaces and compromises the drawn out supportability of these assets.

Contamination: Contamination from modern, farming, and homegrown sources sullies air, water bodies, and soil, influencing the wellbeing of environments and the species inside them.

Intrusive Species: The presentation of non-local species into new conditions can upset local environments, outcompeting nearby species and modifying biological elements.

3. **Arrangements and Systems:**

Preservation: Protection endeavors center around securing and reestablishing normal natural surroundings, rationing imperiled species, and laying out safeguarded regions. These endeavors can assist with protecting biodiversity and natural uprightness.

Supportable Asset The board: Executing manageable fishing, ranger service, and agribusiness practices can guarantee that asset use doesn't drain the climate's ability to recover.

Environment Relief: Diminishing ozone depleting substance emanations through progressing to sustainable power sources, further developing energy effectiveness, and reforestation is basic for moderating environmental change.

Contamination Control: Carrying out stricter ecological guidelines, creating cleaner advancements, and advancing reusing and squander decrease can assist with controlling contamination.

4. **Job of People:**

Supportable Way of life Decisions: People can lessen their biological effect by taking on additional manageable ways of life, like diminishing energy utilization, monitoring water, and limiting waste.

Buyer Decisions: Supporting items and organizations that focus on maintainability and eco-accommodating practices can drive positive change in the commercial center.

Natural Support: People can advocate for ecological assurance by bringing issues to light, partaking in preservation projects, and drawing in with policymakers.

5. **Job of Associations:**

   Corporate Obligation: Organizations and ventures can take on earth capable practices, put resources into supportable stock chains, and limit waste and contamination.

   Examination and Development: Exploration establishments and associations assume a significant part in creating imaginative arrangements and advancements for natural preservation.

6. **Job of Legislatures:**

   Strategy and Guideline: Legislatures can establish and uphold ecological guidelines, set emanation decrease targets, and safeguard regular regions through regulation.

   Worldwide Participation: Cooperative endeavors among countries are vital for address worldwide natural difficulties, for example, environmental change and biodiversity misfortune.

7. **Contextual analyses in Natural Effect:**

   The Incomparable Hindrance Reef: The Incomparable Boundary Reef in Australia is one of the world's most famous biological systems, however it is compromised by coral blanching because of climbing ocean temperatures and sea fermentation. Protection endeavors and worldwide consideration are basic to its conservation.

   Amazon Rainforest: The Amazon rainforest faces huge deforestation because of horticulture, logging, and framework improvement. Preservation drives and reasonable land use rehearses are essential to safeguard this biodiversity area of interest.

8. **Difficulties and Contemplations:**

Transient versus Long haul Interests: Offsetting prompt monetary interests with long haul environmental maintainability can challenge, as certain strategies and practices might influence enterprises and occupations for the time being.

Asset Clashes: Contest for limited assets can prompt struggles, both locally and universally. Overseeing asset designation and access impartially is a complicated test.

Worldwide Disparity: Weak populaces frequently endure the worst part of biological effects, despite the fact that they might have contributed insignificantly to ecological corruption. Value should be viewed as in natural arrangements.

1. Effects on local ecosystems and biodiversity

Neighborhood biological systems and biodiversity are confronting exceptional difficulties because of human exercises. As populaces develop, economies grow, and enterprises advance, the normal world endures the worst part of these changes. This article dives into the massive impacts of human action on nearby environments and biodiversity, the hidden causes, and likely answers for relieve these effects.

1. **The Meaning of Neighborhood Environments and Biodiversity:**
   Environmental Equilibrium: Nearby biological systems assume a urgent part in keeping up with natural equilibrium. They give living space and food to a wide assortment of animal varieties, from microorganisms to huge vertebrates.

   Environment Administrations: These biological systems offer fundamental administrations, for example, fertilization, water filtration, flood control, and environment guideline, which straightforwardly benefit human social orders.

   Social and Stylish Worth: Neighborhood biodiversity adds to social character and offers sporting and tasteful benefit to networks.

2. **Key Impacts on Neighborhood Biological systems and Biodiversity:**
   Natural surroundings Obliteration: Urbanization, farming,

framework improvement, and deforestation lead to territory misfortune and fracture, imperiling various species.

Contamination: Contamination from modern, rural, and home-grown sources defiles neighborhood biological systems, hurting sea-going life, earthbound organic entities, and human wellbeing.

Obtrusive Species: The presentation of non-local species can outcompete and upset neighborhood vegetation, prompting decreases in local biodiversity.

Overexploitation: Over-collecting of assets, including overfishing and unlawful untamed life exchange, can drive neighborhood species to annihilation or risk.

3. **Outcomes of Biological Interruption:**

Loss of Biodiversity: The most immediate outcome is the deficiency of species, decreasing hereditary variety and compromising the strength of environments.

Environment Precariousness: Biological disturbances can prompt irregular characteristics in hunter prey connections, supplement cycling, and generally biological system working.

Modified Biological system Administrations: Changes in nearby environments can disturb the conveyance of biological system administrations, influencing water quality, soil fruitfulness, and harvest fertilization.

4. **Arrangements and Procedures:**

Natural surroundings Preservation: Laying out and keeping up with safeguarded regions, untamed life halls, and environment reclamation ventures can assist with protecting neighborhood biological systems.

Supportable Land Use: Executing feasible land use rehearses, like natural cultivating, agroforestry, and mindful metropolitan preparation, can lessen environment obliteration.

Contamination Control: Upholding severe natural guidelines, creating cleaner advancements, and advancing reusing and squander decrease can assist with controlling contamination.

Intrusive Species The board: Checking and controlling obtrusive species through strategies like destruction, regulation, and rebuilding of local natural surroundings can safeguard neighborhood biodiversity.

5. **Job of People:**

Dependable Utilization: People can go with maintainable decisions in utilization, for example, supporting eco-accommodating items, decreasing waste, and rationing energy.

Natural Stewardship: Participating in neighborhood protection endeavors, partaking in resident science projects, and supporting for ecological assurance can add to biodiversity safeguarding.

6. **Job of Associations:**

Preservation NGOs: Non-legislative associations committed to preservation work to safeguard nearby biological systems and biodiversity through exploration, schooling, and support.

Corporate Obligation: Organizations can take on earth dependable practices, put resources into supportable stockpile chains, and limit waste and contamination.

7. **Job of States:**

Regulation and Authorization: State run administrations can establish and uphold natural guidelines, assign safeguarded regions, and advance supportable land use and asset the executives.

Worldwide Participation: Cooperation among countries is fundamental for address worldwide biodiversity challenges and the security of transient species.

8. **Contextual analyses in Biological Effect on Neighborhood Environments and Biodiversity:**

Amazon Rainforest Deforestation: The Amazon rainforest faces broad deforestation because of logging, agribusiness, and foundation advancement, prompting natural surroundings misfortune and biodiversity decline. Protection endeavors and manageable land use are basic to its conservation.

The African Elephant Emergency: Poaching for ivory and

territory obliteration have driven African elephants to the edge of termination in certain districts. Hostile to poaching endeavors, natural surroundings assurance, and global prohibitions on ivory exchange intend to save this famous species.

9. **Difficulties and Contemplations:**

Momentary versus Long haul Interests: Offsetting quick financial interests with long haul environmental manageability can challenge, as certain approaches and practices might influence enterprises and occupations for the time being.

Worldwide Imbalance: Weak populaces frequently endure the worst part of natural effects, despite the fact that they might have contributed negligibly to ecological debasement. Value should be viewed as in ecological arrangements.

2. Measures taken to minimize harm

Despite heightening ecological difficulties, people, associations, and state run administrations overall are progressively centered around going to lengths to limit mischief to the planet. These proactive endeavors are pointed toward moderating the adverse consequence of human exercises on the climate and encouraging a more feasible conjunction with nature. This paper investigates different measures taken to limit mischief to the climate, featuring their importance and effect.

1. **Meaning of Limiting Damage:**
   Safeguarding Biodiversity: Decreasing mischief to biological systems and environments is critical for protecting biodiversity. Numerous species are in danger of termination because of living space obliteration and contamination.
   Moderating Environmental Change: Limiting ozone depleting substance emanations and advancing energy effectiveness are essential in alleviating environmental change, which has sweeping ramifications for the planet.
   Guaranteeing Asset Supportability: Capable asset the execu-

tives, including water, woodlands, and fisheries, is fundamental to guarantee their accessibility for people in the future.

Safeguarding Human Wellbeing: Natural mischief frequently prompts medical problems in people. Decreasing toxins and foreign substances can emphatically affect general wellbeing.

2. **Key Measures to Limit Damage:**

Sustainable power Reception: Progressing from petroleum derivatives to environmentally friendly power sources, for example, sun oriented, wind, and hydroelectric power, lessens ozone harming substance discharges and battle environmental change.

Maintainable Agribusiness Practices: Practices like natural cultivating, crop revolution, and agroforestry advance soil wellbeing, decrease compound data sources, and cutoff territory obliteration.

Squander Decrease and Reusing: Endeavors to limit squander age and advance reusing lessen the ecological effect of landfills and burning.

Safeguarded Regions and Preservation: Assigning and overseeing safeguarded regions and natural life holds helps defend basic living spaces and undermined species.

Contamination Control: Executing stricter natural guidelines, taking on cleaner advances, and diminishing emanations from ventures assist with controlling contamination.

3. **Job of People:**

Energy Protection: People can preserve energy by utilizing energy-proficient machines, diminishing warming and cooling needs, and switching out lights and hardware when not being used.

Decrease, Reuse, Reuse: Rehearsing the 3Rs - lessen, reuse, and reuse - diminishes squander age and the interest for new assets.

Manageable Transportation: Settling on open transportation, carpooling, trekking, or strolling can diminish individual carbon impressions.

Eco-accommodating Shopper Decisions: Picking eco-accommodating items, supporting reasonable brands, and diminishing single-use plastics are ways people can advance capable utilization.

4. **Job of Associations:**

Corporate Obligation: Organizations can embrace naturally mindful practices, lessen discharges, put resources into maintainable inventory chains, and limit squander.

Exploration and Advancement: Associations can put resources into examination and advancement to foster greener innovations and more manageable practices.

5. **Job of States:**

Strategy and Guideline: State run administrations can order and implement natural guidelines, set discharge decrease targets, and give impetuses to eco-accommodating practices.

Worldwide Participation: Coordinated effort among countries is fundamental for address worldwide ecological difficulties, for example, environmental change and biodiversity misfortune.

6. **Contextual analyses in Limiting Mischief:**

European Association's Outflow Decrease Objectives: The EU has set aggressive emanation decrease targets and executed approaches to progress to environmentally friendly power sources, showing its obligation to relieving environmental change.

Plastic Sack Boycotts: Different nations and urban areas have effectively prohibited or limited the utilization of single-utilize plastic packs, lessening plastic contamination in seas and landfills.

7. **Difficulties and Contemplations:**

Financial Interests: Offsetting monetary interests with natural security can challenge, as certain actions might influence businesses and occupations.

Worldwide Disparity: Weak populaces frequently endure the worst part of natural mischief, despite the fact that they might have contributed negligibly to ecological debasement. Value should be viewed as in ecological arrangements.

B. Sustainability Measures

Manageability measures have turned into a point of convergence in the 21st 100 years as social orders all over the planet wrestle with ecological difficulties, asset exhaustion, and the requirement for a more practical lifestyle. These actions incorporate a scope of procedures and activities pointed toward saving our planet's wellbeing and guaranteeing the prosperity of present and people in the future. In this article, we investigate the meaning of supportability measures, key areas of concentration, and the job of people, associations, and states in propelling manageability.

1. **The Meaning of Maintainability Measures:**
   Ecological Safeguarding: Maintainability measures are fundamental for alleviating ecological corruption, moderating regular assets, and safeguarding environments.

   Financial Practicality: Maintainability advances monetary security and strength by diminishing asset reliance, limiting waste, and encouraging development.

   Social Value: Maintainability guarantees that advantages are appropriated fairly, diminishing variations in admittance to assets and open doors.

   People in the future: Supportability estimates mean to tie down a superior future for a long time into the future by protecting the planet's wellbeing and assets.

2. **Key Areas of Concentration in Maintainability Measures:**
   Environment Activity: Moderating environmental change through the decrease of ozone depleting substance discharges and the progress to environmentally friendly power sources is an essential focal point of supportability measures.

   Asset Protection: Economical asset the executives, including water, backwoods, fisheries, and minerals, is fundamental to stay away from asset consumption.

Biodiversity Preservation: Securing and reestablishing biodiversity through territory protection and capable land use is essential for biological equilibrium.

Squander Decrease and Round Economy: Limiting waste age and advancing a round economy, where assets are reused and reused, diminishes ecological effects.

3. **Measures Taken to Propel Supportability:**

Environmentally friendly power Reception: Changing from petroleum derivatives to sustainable power sources, for example, sun oriented, wind, and hydropower diminishes fossil fuel byproducts and advances manageability.

Supportable Horticulture: Practices like natural cultivating, accuracy farming, and agroforestry upgrade food security while limiting ecological effects.

Green Transportation: Advancing public transportation, electric vehicles, and cycling diminishes outflows from the transportation area.

Productivity Enhancements: Upgrading energy and water proficiency in structures, enterprises, and machines diminishes asset utilization and ecological effect.

4. **Job of People:**

Maintainable Way of life Decisions: People can take on feasible propensities, like diminishing energy utilization, saving water, and limiting waste.

Purchaser Decisions: Supporting items and organizations that focus on maintainability energizes earth dependable practices on the lookout.

Ecological Backing: People can bring issues to light about supportability issues, advocate for strategy changes, and partake in local area drives.

5. **Job of Associations:**

Corporate Obligation: Organizations can embrace naturally capable practices, put resources into maintainable stockpile chains, and limit waste and contamination.

Examination and Advancement: Associations assume a urgent part in creating imaginative arrangements and innovations that advance maintainability.

6. **Job of Legislatures:**

Strategy and Guideline: Legislatures can sanction and authorize ecological guidelines, set outflow decrease targets, and give motivations to supportable practices.

Worldwide Participation: Cooperative endeavors among countries are crucial for address worldwide manageability challenges, for example, environmental change and asset the board.

7. **Contextual analyses in Maintainability Measures:**

Nordic Nations' Sustainable power Progress: Nordic nations like Denmark and Sweden have taken critical steps in changing to sustainable power sources, diminishing their fossil fuel byproducts and dependence on petroleum products.

Zero-Squander Urban areas: Urban communities like San Francisco, California, and Kamikatsu, Japan, have carried out extensive waste decrease and reusing programs, taking a stab at zero waste.

8. **Difficulties and Contemplations:**

Monetary Compromises: Offsetting manageability with financial interests can challenge, as certain actions might influence businesses and occupations temporarily.

Value and Access: Guaranteeing that supportability estimates benefit all populaces and don't excessively trouble weak networks is fundamental.

1. **Long-term sustainability and water management**

Water, frequently alluded to as the "mixture of life," is a fundamental asset for human endurance and the prosperity of our planet. However, notwithstanding its principal significance, we wind up confronting an extraordinary test - the supportable administration of water assets in the long haul. As the total populace proceeds to develop and environmental change compounds water shortage, resolving this issue has turned into an earnest worldwide need.

The Developing Water Emergency

The worldwide water emergency is a mind boggling and diverse issue that appears in different ways. One of the most major problems is water shortage, influencing billions of individuals around the world. As per the Unified Countries, north of 2 billion individuals presently live in regions with high water pressure, and this number is projected to ascend because of populace development and changing utilization designs.

Environmental change assumes a critical part in worsening water shortage. Climbing temperatures and adjusted precipitation examples can disturb the regular water cycle, prompting delayed dry spells in certain locales and more serious precipitation in others. These super climate occasions strain water assets as well as increment the gamble of flooding and water-related debacles.

The Requirement for Long haul Maintainability

To address the worldwide water emergency, a shift towards long haul maintainability in water the board is basic. Manageability in this setting implies involving water assets such that addresses the issues of the present without compromising the capacity of people in the future to address their own issues. Accomplishing this objective requires a complex methodology that thinks about biological, social, and financial aspects.

1. **Protection and Proficiency**

    Protection and productivity measures are significant for practical water the board. Diminishing water squander through better rural practices, modern cycles, and homegrown water use can assist with guaranteeing that accessible water assets are utilized all the more actually. Innovations, for example, trickle water system and brilliant water meters can add to these endeavors.

2. **Foundation Venture**

Putting resources into water foundation is one more fundamental part of long haul maintainability. This incorporates constructing and keeping up with dams, repositories, and wastewater treatment plants. Updating and modernizing these frameworks can build their effectiveness and versatility, assisting communities with better enduring the effects of environmental change.

3. **Environment Rebuilding**

Biological systems assume an imperative part in controlling water accessibility and quality. Reestablishing and safeguarding wetlands, backwoods, and watersheds can assist with keeping up with regular water balance and decrease the gamble of floods and dry seasons. Sound environments likewise add to water decontamination, making water sources more secure and more dependable.

4. **Incorporated Water Asset The board**

Incorporated Water Asset The executives (IWRM) is a comprehensive methodology that perceives the interconnectedness of water sources, including surface water, groundwater, and water. IWRM underscores cooperation among different partners, like states, networks, and businesses, to foster supportable water arrangements and practices.

5. **Environment Transformation**

Given the continuous effects of environmental change, it is fundamental to adjust to changing water conditions. This includes creating methodologies to adapt to additional
successive and serious dry seasons and floods. Environment tough framework, water capacity, and debacle readiness are all essential for viable transformation endeavors.

6. **Instruction and Mindfulness**

Advancing water education and mindfulness is pivotal for long haul manageability. Teaching general society about water protection, contamination anticipation, and the significance of safeguarding environments can prompt more mindful water use at the individual and local area levels.

Global Participation

The worldwide idea of the water emergency requires global participation. Transboundary streams and springs frequently cross numerous nations, making it fundamental for countries to team up on reasonable water the board. Associations like the Assembled Countries and the World Water Committee work with discourse and discussion among nations, assisting with forestalling clashes over water assets.

Difficulties to Long haul Supportability

1. **Political and Institutional Boundaries**

   Political and institutional snags frequently block the reception of maintainable water arrangements. Momentary political needs might eclipse long haul arranging, prompting deficient interest in water framework and preservation endeavors.

2. **Absence of Financing**

   Reasonable water the executives requires critical monetary assets. Numerous locales, especially in the creating scene, come up short on financing expected to put resources into water framework and protection measures.

3. **Information and Observing**

   Exact information on water accessibility, quality, and use are fundamental for informed direction. Notwithstanding, in numerous locales, information assortment and observing frameworks are deficient, making it trying to foster successful water the board techniques.

4. **Value and Access**

Guaranteeing evenhanded admittance to perfect and safe water for everything is a principal part of maintainability. Differences in admittance to water assets, especially in underestimated networks, should be addressed to accomplish long haul maintainability.

2. Balancing development and ecology

In our quest for monetary turn of events and cultural advancement, we frequently wind up at a junction where the interests of human progression conflict with those of natural safeguarding. This fragile harmony among improvement and biology is a test of principal significance in our cutting edge world, where the outcomes of disregarding the climate can be serious and irreversible. Striking the right balance between these two apparently restricting powers isn't just fundamental for the prosperity of our planet yet additionally for the drawn out thriving of humankind.

The Situation of Improvement

Monetary improvement is verifiably imperative for working on expectations for everyday comforts, diminishing neediness, and upgrading generally speaking personal satisfaction. Framework projects, industrialization, urbanization, and innovative headways have added to exceptional advancement across the globe. Nonetheless, the speed and nature of this improvement have frequently come at a high ecological expense.

Ecological Debasement

Uncontrolled improvement oftentimes prompts natural debasement. Deforestation, contamination, territory annihilation, and over-extraction of regular assets are a portion of the results that compromise biological systems, jeopardize species, and upset the fragile equilibrium of nature. This corruption harms the climate as well as influences human wellbeing and prosperity through air and water contamination and the deficiency of fundamental biological system administrations.

Environmental Change

One of the most squeezing difficulties within recent memory, environmental change, is fundamentally determined by human exercises connected with advancement, like the consuming of non-renewable energy sources, deforestation, and modern cycles. The results of unrestrained environmental change, including more continuous and serious climate occasions, rising ocean levels, and disturbances to horticulture, represent an immediate danger to human social orders.

The Requirement for Environmental Protection

Nature, the investigation of the connections between living organic entities and their current circumstance, stresses the many-sided interconnectedness of all life structures on The planet. Saving biological equilibrium doesn't involve decision; it is a basic for supporting life on our planet. Here are a few key justifications for why environment should be a focal thought chasing improvement:

1. **Biological system Administrations**
   Biological systems offer fundamental types of assistance to mankind, like clean air and water, fertilization of yields, and guideline of environment. Upsetting these administrations can have desperate ramifications for human prosperity and the worldwide economy.

2. **Biodiversity**
   Biodiversity is a proportion of the assortment and changeability of life on The planet. It guarantees biological system strength and flexibility and gives hereditary assets to farming and medication. The deficiency of biodiversity compromises our capacity to address future difficulties, including infection flare-ups and food security.

3. **Environment Relief and Variation**
   Solid environments assume a vital part in moderating environmental change by engrossing carbon dioxide and managing temperature and weather conditions. Saving woods, wetlands, and seas is fundamental for alleviating environmental change and adjusting to its effects.

4. **Moral Obligation**

As stewards of the planet, we have a moral obligation to secure and protect the regular world. Numerous native societies have long perceived this obligation, accentuating concordance with nature and regard for every single living being.

Methodologies for Adjusting Advancement and Biology

Adjusting improvement and environment requires an insightful and complex methodology that looks to accommodate human advancement with biological safeguarding. Here are a few systems to assist with accomplishing this balance:

1. **Feasible Turn of events**

   Embracing the idea of supportable advancement is essential. This involves addressing the necessities of the present without compromising the capacity of people in the future to address their own issues. Manageable advancement intends to incorporate financial, social, and ecological contemplations into dynamic cycles.

2. **Protection and Rebuilding**

   Protecting existing normal living spaces and reestablishing de-based ones are essential moves toward adjusting improvement and nature. Preservation endeavors can incorporate laying out safeguarded regions, making untamed life hallways, and carrying out reforestation and wetland reclamation projects.

3. **Green Advancements**

   Headways in innovation can uphold both turn of events and environmental safeguarding. Putting resources into green advances, for example, sustainable power sources, manageable horticulture rehearses, and eco-accommodating transportation choices, can decrease natural effects while advancing monetary development.

4. **Biological system based Approaches**

   Environment based approaches consider the job of biological systems being developed preparation. These methodologies perceive the worth of unblemished biological systems in offering types of assistance like flood control, water filtration, and environment guideline.

5. **Ecological Guidelines and Requirement**

   States and administrative bodies assume a critical part in guaranteeing that improvement exercises stick to ecological norms. Executing and implementing guidelines that limit contamination, safeguard normal environments, and advance economical asset the board are fundamental for protecting nature.

6. **Public Mindfulness and Instruction**

Raising public mindfulness and instructing networks about the significance of environment and economical improvement can cultivate a feeling of obligation and aggregate activity. Informed residents are bound to help approaches and drives that focus on natural protection.

Chapter 6

Challenges and Controversies

In a quickly impacting world portrayed by mechanical headways, social moves, and developing international scenes, difficulties and contentions flourish. These diverse issues incorporate a wide exhibit of points, from governmental issues and morals to innovation and climate. This paper digs into probably the most squeezing difficulties and contentions confronting society today, investigating their beginnings, suggestions, and likely arrangements.

1. **Political Difficulties and Debates**
   Polarization and Populism
   Starting points: Political polarization has strengthened in numerous popular governments around the world, driven by factors like monetary disparity, social personality, and media discontinuity. Libertarian developments frequently exploit these divisions for political increase.
   Suggestions: Polarization can impede successful administration, as gatherings focus on sectarian interests over split the difference. Populism can prompt troublesome approaches and disintegration of majority rule standards.

Arrangements: Advancing media proficiency, discretionary changes, and encouraging valuable discourse can assist with connecting political partitions.

Globalization and Patriotism

Starting points: The strain among globalization and patriotism emerges from the longing for monetary joining and worldwide participation against the background of resurgent patriotism.

Suggestions: Protectionist arrangements can upset worldwide exchange, while worldwide difficulties like environmental change and pandemics require composed reactions.

Arrangements: Offsetting public interests with global collaboration through associations like the Unified Countries and World Exchange Association is vital.

Online protection and Information Security

Beginnings: The expansion of computerized innovation has uncovered people and associations to digital dangers. Information breaks, hacking, and reconnaissance raise critical security concerns.

Suggestions: Cyberattacks can think twice about security and individual protection,

subverting trust in web-based frameworks.

Arrangements: Reinforcing network safety measures, executing powerful information insurance guidelines, and cultivating worldwide participation are fundamental stages.

2. **Moral Difficulties and Debates**

Computerized reasoning and Mechanization

Beginnings: Advances in artificial intelligence and mechanization have raised moral worries about work dislodging, algorithmic predisposition, and the likely abuse of man-made intelligence innovations.

Suggestions: Occupation relocation might worsen pay imbalance, and one-sided calculations can sustain segregation.

Arrangements: Guaranteeing moral man-made intelligence

advancement, advancing

reskilling and upskilling projects, and it are fundamental to direct simulated intelligence applications.

Bioethics and Hereditary Designing

Beginnings: Advances in hereditary designing have empowered quality altering and cloning, igniting banters about the moral ramifications of adjusting human qualities.

Suggestions: Moral worries spin around issues like assent, fashioner infants, and unanticipated hereditary results.

Arrangements: Laying out powerful moral rules and administrative structures for hereditary examination and applications is basic.

Ecological Morals and Environmental Change

Beginnings: Environmental change, driven by human exercises, represents an existential danger to the planet, prompting moral predicaments about obligation and feasible practices.

Suggestions: Environmental change compounds worldwide imbalances, compromises biological systems, and jeopardizes people in the future.

Arrangements: Relieving environmental change requires global collaboration, progressing to sustainable power sources, and taking on economical practices.

3. **Innovative Difficulties and Contentions**

Deception and Disinformation

Beginnings: The computerized age has worked with the fast spread of bogus data, deception, and disinformation.

Suggestions: Falsehood can subvert trust in organizations, disintegrate majority rule cycles, and even affect brutality.

Arrangements: Battling falsehood includes media proficiency programs, reality actually taking a look at drives, and dependable online entertainment stages.

Arising Advancements: Biotechnology and Reconnaissance

Beginnings: Arising biotechnologies, as CRISPR, and unavoidable observation advancements, raise worries about protection, morals, and security.

Suggestions: The abuse of biotech could prompt deceptive hereditary changes, while reconnaissance encroaches on common freedoms.

Arrangements: Executing hearty security regulations, cultivating public discussion on biotechnology, and it are fundamental to manage reconnaissance.

Computerized Gap and Admittance to Innovation

Beginnings: The advanced separation is the hole between those with admittance to innovation and the web and those without, frequently affected by financial elements.

Suggestions: Restricted admittance to innovation can compound imbalance, prevent schooling, and cutoff financial open doors.

Arrangements: Extending broadband access, sponsoring innovation for underserved networks, and advancing computerized proficiency can connect the advanced gap.

4. **Ecological Difficulties and Debates**

Biodiversity Misfortune and Protection

Beginnings: Human exercises, including deforestation and living space obliteration, have prompted uncommon paces of species elimination.

Suggestions: Biodiversity misfortune compromises biological system solidness, food security, and human prosperity.

Arrangements: Executing preservation measures, safeguarding normal environments, and advancing supportable land use are indispensable.

Water Shortage and Contamination

Beginnings: Populace development, contamination, and environmental change add to water shortage and tainting, imperiling water assets.

Suggestions: Water shortage can prompt contentions, while dirtied water hurts human wellbeing and environments.

Arrangements: Productive water the executives, contamination control, and interest in water framework are essential.

Energy Progress and Petroleum derivatives

Starting points: The progress from petroleum products to sustainable power sources is vital for battle environmental change however is met with opposition from personal stakes.

Suggestions: Proceeded with dependence on petroleum products speeds up environmental change and harms biological systems.

Arrangements: Speeding up the progress to environmentally friendly power, carrying out carbon evaluating, and supporting green advances are essential advances.

1. Political and Environmental Opposition

In the domain of contemporary worldwide undertakings, political and ecological resistance stands apart as a noticeable and frequently quarrelsome issue. On one hand, political choices and arrangements drive monetary turn of events, foundation tasks, and worldwide relations. On the other, ecological worries, for example,

environmental change, biodiversity misfortune, and asset exhaustion, require critical activity to moderate and adjust to looming emergencies. The interchange between these two circles is portrayed by a steady back-and-forth, as legislatures, activists, ventures, and concerned residents wrestle with the intricacies of adjusting political and natural interests.

The Political Plan and Its Objectives

Political choices are much of the time directed by a bunch of contemplations, including monetary development, public safety, and social strength. These goals can once in a while give off an impression of being contrary to ecological targets.

Financial Development: States frequently focus on monetary advancement as a way to work on expectations for everyday comforts, decrease neediness, and upgrade public flourishing. Framework activities, industrialization, and urbanization are indispensable parts of financial development, however they can have antagonistic natural effects, like territory annihilation, contamination, and expanded ozone depleting substance discharges.

Energy Strategy: The energy area assumes a basic part in any country's turn of events, and petroleum products have generally been the essential energy source. Notwithstanding, the extraction and consuming of non-renewable energy sources contribute fundamentally to environmental change and ecological corruption.

Public safety: Public safety concerns, like military readiness and regional debates, can once in a while overshadow ecological protection. Clashes and international pressures can redirect assets and consideration from natural insurance endeavors.

Asset Extraction: The extraction of normal assets, including minerals, lumber, and water, is fundamental for monetary development. In any case, unreasonable asset extraction can prompt deforestation, overfishing, and asset consumption.

Ecological Objectives and Their Difficulties

Ecological resistance emerges from the developing acknowledgment that human exercises have set the planet's environments and environment in danger. The ecological objectives require a change in needs and strategies, regardless of whether it implies testing political choices.

Environmental Change Moderation: The criticalness of relieving environmental change by diminishing ozone harming substance emanations requires a quick progress

away from petroleum products and the reception of sustainable power sources. This change can disturb laid out ventures and financial interests.

Protection of Biodiversity: The deficiency of biodiversity represents a danger to environments, food security, and human prosperity.

Protection endeavors frequently include limiting area use, which can struggle with financial turn of events and land privileges.

Normal Asset Protection: Guaranteeing the economical utilization of regular assets, like freshwater, minerals, and timberlands, is vital for long haul natural manageability. In any case, this requires reconsidering asset serious practices and ventures.

Natural Equity: Ecological resistance regularly converges with issues of civil rights, as minimized networks frequently endure the worst part of ecological corruption and contamination. Tending to these abberations might require reexamining political and monetary designs.

The Perplexing Exchange and Debates

The exchange among political and ecological interests leads to a few discussions and difficulties.

Monetary Interests versus Ecological Worries: Offsetting financial interests with natural worries stays a petulant issue. Projects like oil pipelines and mining tasks frequently produce occupations and income however can prompt ecological harm.

Transient versus Long haul Point of view: Political choices will generally zero in on transient increases, while ecological goals request a drawn out point of view. This pressure can frustrate the reception of practical approaches that focus in the world's prosperity over prompt financial prizes.

Campaigning and Unique Interests: Particular vested parties, including businesses that might be antagonistically impacted by natural guidelines, frequently apply significant impact over political direction, prompting administrative catch and strategy inclination.

Worldwide Collaboration and Environment Strategy: Environmental change is a worldwide test that requires global participation. Talks and arrangements, like the Paris Understanding, feature the difficulties of adjusting public interests and worldwide natural goals.

Public Mindfulness and Backing: Ecological activists and concerned residents assume an essential part in featuring natural issues and constraining states to make a move. Nonetheless, such support can be met with political obstruction and even aggression.

Settling on something worth agreeing on and Arrangements

Strategy Joining: Policymakers ought to plan to incorporate natural contemplations into political choices, underscoring maintainable advancement that offsets monetary development with environmental protection.

Motivations for Green Advancements: States can boost the turn of events and reception of green innovations, for example, environmentally friendly power sources and manageable farming practices, to make mutual benefit situations for both the economy and the climate.

Public Commitment: Public commitment and schooling are fundamental for building support for natural drives. Bringing issues to light about the earnestness of ecological difficulties and their cultural effects can cultivate public interest for capable arrangements.

Worldwide Participation: Environmental change and biodiversity misfortune are worldwide difficulties that require global collaboration. Strategy and arrangements ought to underscore shared liability and aggregate activity.

Straightforwardness and Responsibility: Guaranteeing straightforwardness in political dynamic cycles and considering states responsible for their natural responsibilities can assist with lessening the impact of extraordinary interests.

Natural Effect Appraisals: Carrying out thorough ecological effect evaluations for significant ventures can assist with distinguishing likely ecological dangers and illuminate leaders.

1. **Critics and concerns**

    In practically every feature of human undertaking, from legislative issues and innovation to human expression and social developments, pundits and concerns assume a significant part in forming talk, progress, and responsibility. Pundits offer significant points of view that rock the boat and feature likely deficiencies, while

worries, frequently established in fear or wariness, act as significant preventative banners. This paper dives
into the complex universe of pundits and concerns, investigating their importance, inspirations, and effects on society.

The Job of Pundits

Social Pundits: In the domain of expressions and culture, pundits survey and dissect writing, film, music, and different types of imaginative articulation. Their surveys and evaluates assist with forming popular assessment, give useful criticism to craftsmen, and add to the advancement of social standards and style.

Political Pundits: Political pundits investigate the activities, approaches, and choices of states and political pioneers. They assume a critical part in considering public authorities responsible, pushing for straightforwardness, and guaranteeing the security of common freedoms and vote based values.

Innovation Pundits: In the quickly developing area of innovation, pundits survey the moral, social, and ecological ramifications of advancements like computerized reasoning, biotechnology, and observation. They challenge the possible damages of innovation and call for mindful turn of events and guideline.

Ecological Pundits: Natural pundits center around issues connected with environmental change, biodiversity misfortune, contamination, and asset consumption. They advocate for feasible practices, preservation, and arrangements that address squeezing ecological difficulties.

Social Pundits: Social pundits investigate cultural standards, designs, and imbalances, frequently causing to notice issues like racial treachery, orientation disparity, and monetary inconsistencies. They advance civil rights and correspondence through promotion and mindfulness.

Inspirations and Worries of Pundits

Improvement and Responsibility: Numerous pundits expect to work regarding the matter of their investigate, whether it's a piece of craftsmanship, a strategy, or a cultural standard. They accept that by featuring defects and deficiencies, positive change can happen. Pundits frequently consider themselves to be watchmen of responsibility.

Moral and Moral Worries: Moral contemplations frequently drive analysis. Pundits might be inspired by worries about the moral ramifications of specific activities, strategies, or ways of behaving. For instance, moral worries might underlie evaluates of observation rehearses or naturally harming ventures.

Social and Stylish Qualities: Pundits in the domain of expressions and culture are many times directed by their own qualities and feel. Their scrutinizes are molded by their view of what comprises great craftsmanship, writing, or music. These qualities can be exceptionally abstract.

Backing and Civil rights: Social pundits are driven by a pledge to civil rights and value. They try to reveal insight into cultural treacheries, separation, and disparities, determined to advance positive change and inclusivity.

The Effect of Pundits and Concerns

Illuminating Public Talk: Pundits add to informed public talk by offering different viewpoints and experiences. Their surveys and investigations can teach the general population and energize decisive reasoning.

Responsibility and Change: Pundits frequently act as guard dogs, holding people, establishments, and legislatures responsible for their activities. Their investigation can prompt approach changes, further developed rehearses, and expanded straightforwardness.

Social Advancement: Social pundits impact creative and social standards. Their surveys and studies can influence the gathering and improvement of imaginative works, forming the course of creative developments and patterns.

Social Change: Social pundits play played urgent parts in driving social change from the beginning of time. Developments for social liberties, orientation correspondence, and natural protection have been impelled by the studies of cultural standards and treacheries.

Discussions Encompassing Pundits and Concerns

Subjectivity: Pundits' appraisals are many times abstract, formed by private predispositions, tastes, and convictions. This subjectivity can prompt conflicts and disagreements regarding the legitimacy of their studies.

Adverse consequence: A few pundits might zero in fundamentally on cynicism and scrutinize without offering helpful arrangements. This can cultivate a culture of pessimism and frustrate progress.

2. **The project's response to controversies**

In the present interconnected and various world, ventures of assorted types, whether they are in the domains of business, legislative issues, or social drives, frequently wind up exploring through discussions and difficulties. These discussions can emerge from different sources, for example, clashing partner interests, moral problems, or unanticipated impediments. What a venture answers debates can essentially mean for its prosperity, notoriety, and long haul manageability. This paper investigates the systems and contemplations that undertakings can utilize to address and oversee discussions successfully.

Grasping the Idea of Debates

Prior to digging into techniques, getting a handle on the idea of controversies is fundamental. Discussions commonly arise when there is a disparity of sentiments, interests, or values. A few normal wellsprings of venture related contentions include:

Partner Clashes: Various partners, including financial backers, workers, clients, and networks, may have clashing interests or assumptions about the task's results and effects.

Moral and Moral Problems: Ventures might confront moral situations connected with issues like ecological supportability, social obligation, or fair work rehearses.

Political and Administrative Difficulties: Unofficial laws, strategies, and political elements can present vulnerabilities and debates, especially in enterprises subject to broad guideline.

Mechanical Dangers: Activities that include state of the art innovations or logical headways might confront concerns connected with wellbeing, security, or unexpected results.

Market and Monetary Elements: Monetary vacillations, market rivalry, and inventory network disturbances can prompt discussions encompassing venture feasibility and monetary dangers.

Techniques for Tending to Discussions

Partner Commitment and Correspondence:

Undivided attention: Undertakings ought to proactively draw in with partners, pay attention to their interests, and try to figure out their points of view. This can assist with distinguishing potential debates right off the bat.

Straightforwardness: Straightforward correspondence about project objectives, progress, and difficulties can assemble entrust with partners. Straightforwardness can assist with dissipating mistaken assumptions and confusions.

Normal Updates: Giving partners customary updates on project improvements and resolving various forms of feedback speedily shows a guarantee to straightforwardness and responsibility.

Risk Evaluation and Moderation:

Possibility Arranging: Recognizing expected debates and creating emergency courses of action for addressing them is a proactive way to deal with risk the board. Having alternate courses of action set up can assist with limiting the effect of startling difficulties.

Natural and Social Effect Appraisals: Tasks with potential ecological or social effects ought to direct intensive evaluations to grasp the likely dangers and foster relief measures.

Administrative Consistence: Guaranteeing severe consistence with every pertinent guideline and regulations can assist with forestalling administrative contentions and legitimate difficulties.

Moral Independent direction:

Morals Councils: A few undertakings, especially those including logical examination or novel innovations, may profit from laying out morals panels or warning sheets to give direction on moral contemplations.

Moral Rules: Obviously characterized moral rules can assist with projecting groups explore complex choices by giving a system to assessing moral ramifications.

Versatile Administration:

Adaptability: Undertakings ought to be versatile and receptive to evolving conditions. Being willing to change project plans and systems when vital can assist with staying away from contentions coming about because of rigidity.

Gaining from Errors: Undertakings ought to see debates as any open doors for learning and improvement. Examining past contentions can prompt better dynamic later on.

Advertising and Media The board:

Media Relations: Tasks ought to have a thoroughly examined media methodology to oversee public insights and reactions. Imparting the undertaking's objectives and advantages can assist with moderating negative inclusion.

Emergency Correspondence: in case of a discussion, undertakings ought to have an emergency correspondence plan set up to resolve issues immediately, give exact data, and oversee advertising really.

Local area Commitment:

Local area Effort: For projects with nearby or local area influences, drawing in with impacted networks and tending to their interests can construct backing and generosity.

Social Obligation: Ventures ought to consider the social obligations related with their exercises and, when possible, make moves to help the networks where they work.

Cooperation and Organizations:

Partner Joint effort: Teaming up with partners, including non-administrative associations (NGOs) and local gatherings, can assist with tending to discussions through discourse and participation.

Industry Collusions: Joining industry unions and associations can give assets and backing to address shared difficulties and discussions.

Contextual analyses in Discussion The board

Tesla and Electric Vehicle Contentions: Tesla, a main electric vehicle producer, confronted debates connected with vehicle security, creation deferrals, and Chief Elon Musk's public assertions. The organization answered by further developing security highlights, expanding creation limit, and improving correspondence with partners.

The Dakota Access Pipeline: This pipeline project confronted broad contention and fights because of natural and social worries. To address the debates, the venture drew in with Native people group, led extra ecological evaluations, and consented to administrative necessities.

Coronavirus Immunization Advancement: The fast turn of events and conveyance of Coronavirus antibodies raised worries about security, viability, and evenhanded access. Immunization designers tended to discussions by leading thorough clinical

preliminaries, teaming up with worldwide wellbeing associations, and giving straightforward data about antibody improvement and dissemination.

B. Technical Challenges

In the quickly developing scene of innovation, specialized difficulties are a steady presence. These difficulties emerge from the tenacious quest for advancement, the intricacies of arising innovations, and the consistently expanding requests for proficiency and dependability. Exploring these specialized difficulties is fundamental for the advancement of society and industry. In this paper, we'll investigate the idea of specialized difficulties, their importance, and the techniques utilized to conquer them.

Grasping Specialized Difficulties

Intricacy and Scale: Numerous specialized difficulties originate from the rising intricacy and size of present day advances. As frameworks become more unpredictable, overseeing and keeping up with them become really difficult.

Interoperability: Guaranteeing that various innovations can co-operate flawlessly is an industrious test. Contrary qualities between programming, equipment, and conventions can prompt shortcomings and framework disappointments.

Security and Protection: With the multiplication of computerized frameworks and information, network safety and security concerns are fundamental. Safeguarding touchy data and defending against digital dangers is a continuous test.

Asset Imperatives: Limitations on assets, for example, restricted handling power, memory, and transmission capacity, can thwart the exhibition and versatility of innovations.

Administrative Consistence: Quick mechanical progressions frequently outperform administrative systems, making provokes for businesses to adjust to new guidelines while keeping up with consistence.

Maintainability: Creating innovations that are ecologically economical is a developing test, given the rising spotlight on diminishing carbon impressions and limiting electronic waste.

Meaning of Specialized Difficulties

Advancement and Progress: Beating specialized difficulties is fundamental for driving development and mechanical advancement. Forward leaps frequently happen when groups tackle complex specialized issues.

Monetary Intensity: Businesses that effectively address specialized difficulties can acquire an upper hand. Advancement and specialized greatness add to monetary development.

Quality and Dependability: Specialized difficulties influence the quality and unwavering quality of items and administrations. Tending to these difficulties is vital for meeting shopper assumptions and guaranteeing wellbeing.

Security and Protection: Inability to address security and security difficulties can bring about information breaks, monetary misfortunes, and harm to notoriety.

Ecological Effect: Manageable innovation arrangements are fundamental for decreasing the natural impression of enterprises and limiting the effect on environments.

Systems for Beating Specialized Difficulties

Innovative work:

Interest in Exploration: Dispensing assets for innovative work endeavors is significant for remaining in front of specialized difficulties. These ventures can prompt forward leaps in innovation.

Cooperative Exploration: Teaming up with scholarly foundations, research associations, and industry friends can give new experiences and aptitude to handle complex specialized issues.

Interdisciplinary Groups:

Different Ranges of abilities: As specialized difficulties become progressively mind boggling, gathering interdisciplinary groups with an assorted scope of abilities and mastery can be exceptionally viable in tracking down arrangements.

Cross-utilitarian Cooperation: Advancing coordinated effort between engineers, researchers, planners, and business specialists can prompt comprehensive arrangements that think about specialized, social, and financial variables.

Prototyping and Testing:

Prototyping: Building models and leading iterative testing is essential for distinguishing and tending to specialized imperfections from the get-go in the advancement cycle.

Recreation and Demonstrating: High level reenactment and displaying apparatuses empower specialists to foresee how frameworks will perform under different circumstances, supporting critical thinking.

Persistent Learning and Preparing:

Representative Turn of events: Putting resources into preparing and improvement programs for workers helps stay up with the latest and cultivates a culture of development.

Information Sharing: Empowering information sharing inside an association can assist with spreading skill and answers for specialized difficulties.

Administrative Consistence:

Proactive Commitment: Drawing in with administrative bodies right off the bat in the improvement cycle can work with consistence and forestall exorbitant postponements.

Versatile Consistence: Creating frameworks and cycles that can adjust to changing guidelines is fundamental in quick ventures.

Maintainable Practices:

Eco-plan: Integrating natural contemplations into the plan period of innovation advancement can prompt more reasonable items and cycles.

Asset Effectiveness: Executing asset productive practices, for example, energy-saving advancements and waste decrease measures, can moderate natural effect.

Security and Protection Measures:

Network safety Conventions: Carrying out powerful network protection conventions and encryption measures can shield frameworks and touchy information from dangers.

Security by Configuration: Planning innovation frameworks in view of security, including information anonymization and client assent, is significant for safeguarding client data.

Contextual analyses in Beating Specialized Difficulties

SpaceX and Reusable Rockets: SpaceX, drove by Elon Musk, confronted the specialized test of decreasing the expense of room travel. They created reusable rocket innovation, empowering rockets to get back to Earth and be relaunched. This advancement essentially decreased send off costs and made space travel more open.

5G Organization Sending: The arrangement of 5G organizations presented specialized difficulties connected with network thickness, information paces, and energy proficiency. Cooperation between media communications organizations and analysts brought about the improvement of cutting edge recieving wire advances and organization enhancement arrangements.

Electric Vehicle Reach and Charging: Electric vehicles (EVs) confronted specialized difficulties connected with restricted battery range and charging foundation. Progressing research in battery innovation and the extension of charging networks have added to the development of the EV market.

1. **Lessons learned and innovations**

   In the always developing scene of human undertaking, the excursion is stamped by the objective as well as by the illustrations advanced en route. Chasing progress, whether in the domains of science, innovation, business, or self-improvement, each step in the right direction is a consequence of the two victories and disappointments. Examples learned give the fruitful ground to development to flourish, prompting extraordinary forward leaps that shape what's to come. This paper investigates the complex connection between examples learned and developments, delineating how they are indistinguishable accomplices in the excursion of human progression.

   Illustrations Took in: The Cauldron of Development

   Illustrations learned are the foundation of human advancement. They rise out of encounters that test our capacities, challenge our presumptions, and frequently compel us to adjust. These illustrations can be drawn from both achievement and disappointment, each granting its special insight. The meaning of these examples lies in their capacity to shape our activities and choices later on.

   Disappointment as an Impetus: Disappointment is many times the most powerful instructor. The aggravation of rout makes permanent imprints, pushing us to break down our missteps and look for better techniques. Developments brought into the world from disappointment are a demonstration of human flexibility and versatility. For example, Thomas Edison's various endeavors to make a functioning light just prevailed after a

huge number of disappointments. Every disappointment showed him what wouldn't work, eventually prompting perhaps of the most extraordinary development ever.

Accomplishment as an Establishment: Achievement, then again, fabricates the establishment whereupon developments are built. Achievement approves our endeavors and urges us to drive further. Nonetheless, analyzing achievement, understanding the components that prompted it is similarly significant. The illustrations gained from fruitful undertakings help refine and work on existing advancements. Apple's persevering quest for greatness in its items and client experience is an illustration of how achievement can be an impetus for persistent development.

Developments: The Products of Learning

Developments are the substantial results of examples learned. They are the encapsulation of our inventive and critical thinking skills, filled by the bits of knowledge acquired from previous encounters. Advancements come in different structures, from mechanical leap forwards to novel business procedures, and, surprisingly, individual changes.

Mechanical Progressions: In the domain of science and innovation, illustrations gained from past trials, triumphs, and disappointments act as building blocks for pivotal developments. The improvement of the web, for instance, is a consequence of many years of illustrations learned in PC organizing, information transmission, and convention plan. Advancements like the Internet, which altered data sharing, were just conceivable due to this amassed information.

Business Systems: In the business world, developments

frequently emerge from examples found out about market elements, client conduct, and functional efficiencies. Organizations like Amazon have changed the retail scene by continually enhancing their plans of action in view of client criticism and market experiences. The example of client centricity has been critical to their prosperity.

Self-awareness and Improvement: On an individual level, examples gained from life encounters add to self-improvement and personal growth. Development in this setting includes tracking down better approaches to explore difficulties and lead a really satisfying life. For example, somebody who has gained from previous slip-ups and grew better critical thinking abilities is improving in their own life by making a more sure future.

The Harmonious Relationship

The connection between illustrations learned and developments is harmonious, with each taking care of into the other. Advancements are in many cases the immediate aftereffect of illustrations learned, yet developments can likewise prompt new examples and bits of knowledge.

Iterative Improvement: Advancements are seldom wonderful all along. They are refined and enhanced over the long haul in light of criticism and certifiable utilization. These refinements comprise new illustrations realized, which, thusly, lead to additional advancements. This iterative cycle is the driving force of progress. For instance, the development of cell phones from inconvenient early models to smooth, strong gadgets is the consequence of a constant pattern of development and learning.

Unseen side-effects: Developments can likewise lead to potentially negative results or examples. For example, the inescapable reception of web-based entertainment stages achieved a large group of unanticipated difficulties, including issues connected with protection, falsehood, and psychological wellness. These results have constrained society to learn significant illustrations about the dependable utilization of innovation, which might illuminate future developments in computerized correspondence and morals.

2. Future-proofing the Kaleshwaram Project

The Kaleshwaram Lift Water system Venture, situated in the Indian province of Telangana, is one of the most aggressive water framework projects on the planet. Intended to tackle the Godavari Stream's waters for water system and drinking purposes, the venture plans to change the bone-dry terrains of Telangana into fruitful farming fields and give genuinely necessary drinking water to its developing populace. In any case, in a quickly impacting world set apart by environment changeability and expanding water shortage, it is basic to future-confirmation the Kaleshwaram Undertaking to guarantee its drawn out maintainability and viability.

Understanding the Kaleshwaram Undertaking

The Kaleshwaram Venture includes the development of an organization of repositories, passages, and siphon houses to redirect water from the Godavari Stream and transport it to different pieces of Telangana. It includes three principal parts: the Medigadda Torrent, the Annaram Blast, and the Sundilla Flood, alongside a few other more modest designs. The undertaking can possibly essentially build the flooded region in the state and give drinking water to a huge number of individuals.

Difficulties and Contemplations for Future-Sealing

Environmental Change: Environmental change represents a huge danger to the venture's drawn out suitability. Changing precipitation designs, expanded temperatures, and modified hydrological cycles can affect the accessibility of water in the Godavari Stream. To future-evidence the undertaking, environment strong procedures should be taken on, for example, standard environment demonstrating, versatile administration rehearses, and the advancement of elective water sources.

Water Shortage: As populace development and urbanization proceed, the interest for water in Telangana is probably going to increment.

To guarantee water security for a long time into the future, the task should integrate systems for proficient water use, including water reusing, water collecting, and the advancement of water-saving rural practices.

Natural Worries: The Kaleshwaram Undertaking's effect on the climate, especially on environments along the Godavari Waterway, involves concern. Future-sealing the task includes limiting environmental disturbances through measures like living space rebuilding, fish relocation pathways, and supportable water discharge rehearses that copy regular stream systems.

Mechanical Progressions: Embracing the most recent innovative headways in water the executives is essential for future-sealing the task. Integrating continuous information observing, remote detecting, and progressed investigation can assist with advancing water allotment and circulation, making the venture more proficient and versatile to evolving conditions.

Procedures for Future-Sealing

Enhance Water Sources: Over-dependence on a solitary stream framework can be unsafe, particularly notwithstanding environment vulnerability. Future-sealing the Kaleshwaram Task ought to include investigating extra water sources, for example, groundwater re-energize, interlinking of streams, and desalination, to supply guarantee a more hearty and differentiated water.

Execute Water Protection Measures: Empowering water preservation rehearses at both the farming and civil levels is fundamental. Ranchers can be instructed on proficient water system strategies like dribble and sprinkler frameworks, while metropolitan regions can advance water-saving machines and water reaping.

Versatile Administration: The task ought to take on a versatile administration approach that considers adaptability in answering evolving conditions. Normal appraisals and changes in accordance with the venture's activities, in light of environment information and water accessibility, will be urgent for its drawn out progress.

Biological system Reclamation: To relieve ecological effects, the task ought to incorporate far reaching environment rebuilding plans. This might include the making of untamed life passageways, fish stepping stools, and reforestation endeavors along the Godavari Stream.

Put resources into Exploration and Development: Persistent interest in examination and advancement is fundamental for the undertaking's future-sealing. This incorporates the improvement of prescient models, high level water decontamination advancements, and economical horticultural practices custom-made to the district's changing water elements.

Public Mindfulness and Support: Drawing in neighborhood networks and partners in the undertaking's preparation and dynamic cycles is essential. Their feedback can give important experiences and assist with building a feeling of pride, guaranteeing the venture's drawn out progress.

7

Chapter 7

Success Stories

Examples of overcoming adversity are something beyond accounts of accomplishment; they are the narratives of human steadiness, inventiveness, and flexibility. These accounts impact us since they address the victory of the human soul despite everything. In this assortment of examples of overcoming adversity, we dig into the lives and excursions of people and associations who resisted difficulties, sought after their fantasies, and made exceptional progress. These accounts act as signals of motivation, directing us through the most obscure of times and advising us that earnestly and difficult work, we can defeat any snag and arrive at our maximum capacity.

1. **Individual Examples of overcoming adversity**
   The Ascent of Elon Musk: From PayPal to Mars Colonization
   Elon Musk, the visionary business person behind SpaceX, Tesla, and a few other weighty organizations, is a demonstration of daring desire. This example of overcoming adversity follows Musk's excursion from helping to establish PayPal to spearheading reusable rocket innovation at SpaceX, reforming the electric vehicle industry with Tesla, and focusing on colonizing Mars.

Musk's determined quest for his objectives and readiness to take on apparently outlandish difficulties have made him a symbol of advancement and steadiness.

Oprah Winfrey: From Destitution to News Investor

Oprah Winfrey's biography is a strong story of win over difficulty. Naturally introduced to neediness and confronting various difficulties, she rose to become perhaps of the most powerful medium characters on the planet. This example of overcoming adversity investigates Oprah's initial battles, her forward leap in the broadcast business, and her change into a donor and backer for schooling and civil rights.

Malala Yousafzai: The Voice for Young ladies' Schooling

Malala Yousafzai's story is one of striking mental fortitude and versatility. Shot by the Taliban for supporting young ladies' schooling in Pakistan, Malala made due as well as proceeded with her main goal with much more noteworthy assurance. She turned into the most youthful Nobel laureate and a worldwide image of the battle for orientation

correspondence in training. This example of overcoming adversity features her relentless obligation to instruction and strengthening.

Scratch Vujicic: Conquering Handicaps with Inspiration

Scratch Vujicic was brought into the world without arms and legs, confronting an existence of significant actual difficulties. Be that as it may, he transformed his misfortune into a wellspring of motivation for millions around the world. This example of overcoming adversity narratives Scratch's excursion of self-acknowledgment, his promotion for individuals with handicaps, and his wonderful accomplishments as a powerful orator and creator.

2. **Business and Enterprising Examples of overcoming adversity**
   Apple Inc.: From Carport Startup to Trillion-Dollar Realm
   Apple Inc's. venture from a little carport startup to becoming

one of the world's most important and compelling innovation organizations is an exemplary example of overcoming adversity. This account investigates the creative items, visionary initiative of Steve Occupations, and the organization's getting through obligation to plan greatness and client experience that impelled it to progress.

Amazon: The Everything Store

Jeff Bezos' creation, Amazon, began as a web-based book shop yet developed into a worldwide internet business and innovation goliath. This example of overcoming adversity digs into Amazon's persistent spotlight on client centricity, its advancements in planned operations and distributed computing, and its extraordinary effect on ventures going from retail to diversion.

Alibaba: Connecting the Advanced Separation in China

Jack Mama's Alibaba Gathering is a perfect representation of how assurance and versatility can prompt innovative achievement. This example of overcoming adversity investigates Alibaba's excursion from a little loft in Hangzhou to turning into a worldwide online business force to be reckoned with, as well as its part in connecting the computerized partition in China.

3. **Social and Compassionate Examples of overcoming adversity**
   Nelson Mandela: The Victory of Compromise

Nelson Mandela's biography is an image of trust, compromise, and win over persecution. This example of overcoming adversity relates his battle against politically-sanctioned racial segregation in South Africa, his long detainment, and his

astounding excursion to turning into the country's most memorable dark president. Mandela's heritage fills in as a guide of pardoning, solidarity, and civil rights.

Greta Thunberg: Youth Activism for Environmental Change

Greta Thunberg, a Swedish youngster, started a worldwide youth development pushing for environment activity. Her story features the force of youthful voices in molding the world's reaction to environmental change. This example of overcoming adversity investigates Greta's energy for natural activism and her capacity to activate a large number of youthful activists around the world.

4. **Logical and Mechanical Examples of overcoming adversity**

The Human Genome Task: Deciphering the Plan of Life

The Human Genome Task was a great logical undertaking to guide and succession the whole human genome. This example of overcoming adversity uncovers the cooperative endeavors of researchers around the world, their leap forwards in genomics, and the significant effect of this venture on medication, hereditary qualities, and our comprehension of human science.

SpaceX's Mars Colonization Vision: Making People Multiplanetary

SpaceX, drove by Elon Musk, is determined to make mankind a multiplanetary animal groups by colonizing Mars. This example of overcoming adversity digs into the organization's aggressive objectives, its developments in rocket innovation, and its vision for the fate of room investigation.

1. **Personal Narratives**

Individual accounts are the narratives we educate ourselves as well as other people regarding our lives, encounters, and characters. They are the strings that wind around together the texture of our reality, molding how we might interpret what our identity is and the way in which we connect with our general surroundings. These accounts are not simple memories; they are the apparatuses through which we figure out our past, characterize our present, and imagine our future. In this investigation of individual accounts, we dive into their importance, impact, and the manners by which they can enable people to create their own one of a kind biographies.

1. **The Meaning of Individual Stories**

   Self-Character and Conviction Frameworks: Individual stories are the structure blocks of our self-personality. They assist us with building a feeling of what our identity is by sorting out our recollections, encounters, and convictions into an intelligent story. For instance, somebody who approaches their encounters as a progression of wins over misfortune might foster areas of strength for an of flexibility and self-viability.

   Feeling of Progression: Individual stories give a feeling of congruity in our lives. They draw an obvious conclusion regarding our past, present, and future, permitting us to perceive how our encounters have formed us and how they might keep on affecting us. This feeling of coherence can give solidness and motivation, even despite life's vulnerabilities.

   Correspondence and Association: Individual stories are not simply interior develops; they are likewise method for correspondence. Imparting our accounts to others permits us to interface on a profound, close to home level. Our accounts assist us with connecting with each other, figure out some shared interest, and construct compassion.

2. **The Impact of Individual Stories**

   Inevitable outcomes: Our own stories can become unavoidable outcomes. In the event that somebody reliably lets themselves know that they are not equipped for progress, they may subliminally harm their endeavors. On the other hand, a positive self-story can rouse and engage people to take a stab at their objectives.

   Survival strategies: Individual accounts act as ways of dealing with stress during troublesome times. For example, somebody who has encountered a horrendous mishap might build a story that spotlights on their versatility and capacity to conquer misfortune. This story can give a wellspring of solidarity and strength even with injury.

Social and Social Accounts: Individual stories are not framed in segregation; they are impacted by social and social stories. Society's common tales about progress, orientation jobs, and character can shape our own stories. Perceiving the impact of outside accounts permits people to address and challenge them, preparing for self-awareness and strengthening.

3. **Engaging Through Private Stories**

Reflection and Mindfulness: The most important phase in saddling the force of individual stories is reflection. Finding opportunity to analyze one's own accounts, both positive and negative, can prompt more noteworthy mindfulness. This mindfulness is an establishment whereupon self-improvement and change can be constructed.

Reevaluating and Rescripting: Individual stories are yet to be determined. They can be rethought and rescripted to more readily line up with one's objectives and desires.

For instance, somebody who has consistently seen themselves as a "devotee" can start to tell another story of being a "forerunner really taking shape."

Story Treatment: Account treatment is a remedial methodology that spotlights on assisting people with revising their own accounts in a manner that advances mending and development. Advisors work with clients to investigate and reshape their accounts, giving them new devices for understanding and dealing with their lives.

Positive Representation: Perception procedures, for example, making a dream board or composing a future-centered story, can assist people with showing their ideal results. By picturing their objectives and yearnings, individuals can acquire clearness and inspiration to pursue them.

Strong People group: Sharing individual stories inside steady networks can be a groundbreaking encounter. It permits people to track down approval, sympathy, and motivation from other people who have confronted comparable difficulties and wins. Online gatherings, support gatherings, and narrating occasions give stages to these associations.

1. Stories from beneficiaries

Behind each beneficent drive, government assistance program, or compassionate exertion, there are genuine individuals whose lives have been decidedly influenced. These people, frequently alluded to as recipients, are at the core of the work done by associations, state run administrations, and people devoted to further developing the prosperity of others. In this assortment of stories from recipients, we investigate the significant and frequently extraordinary effect that help and help can have on people and networks, revealing insight into the force of sympathy, liberality, and human association.

1. Instructive Strengthening
1. Amina's Excursion to Education:
Amina, a little kid from a country town in India, was once denied admittance to schooling because of social standards and financial limitations. Be that as it may, a neighborhood non-legislative association (NGO) started a program to advance young ladies' schooling. Through this drive, Amina figured out how to peruse and compose as well as acquired the certainty to challenge cultural assumptions. Today, she fantasies about turning into an educator and engaging different young ladies locally through training.
2. The Grant that Completely changed Ahmed:

Ahmed, a skilled understudy from a low-pay family in Egypt, confronted the gamble of exiting school because of monetary requirements. Nonetheless, a grant program presented by a worldwide establishment furnished him with the monetary help he expected to proceed with his schooling. This help assisted Ahmed with finishing his examinations as well as opened ways to a more promising time to come. He is presently seeking after a degree in medication, with desires to reward his local area.

II. Wellbeing and Clinical Help

1. Maria's Wonder A medical procedure:

Maria, a little kid from a far off town in Honduras, was brought into the world with an inherent heart condition that left her with restricted versatility and a distressing guess. Be that as it may, a clinical mission coordinated by a worldwide wellbeing association carried a group of gifted specialists to her town. Because of their skill and the liberality of contributors, Maria went through a day to day existence saving a medical procedure. Today, she is a functioning and euphoric kid, carrying on with a solid life liberated from the weight of her condition.

2. The Portable Center that Saved Hassan's Sight:

Hassan, an older man in an evacuee camp in Syria, was experiencing disintegrating vision yet had no admittance to clinical consideration. A philanthropic association set up a portable eye facility in the camp, offering free eye tests and medical procedures. Hassan got the treatment he wanted, and his sight was reestablished. Yet again this basic thoughtful gesture changed his life, permitting him to see the essences of his friends and family.

III. Monetary Strengthening

1. Sarah's Enterprising Excursion:

Sarah, a single parent of two in Kenya, battled to earn enough to get by selling vegetables in her neighborhood market. Through a microfinance program, she got a little credit and preparing in business the board. Sincerely and difficult work, Sarah extended her little vegetable stand into a flourishing supermarket. Her prosperity worked on her family's everyday environments as well as roused different ladies locally to seek after business.

2. From Vagrancy to Homeownership:

John, a U.S. military veteran, confronted vagrancy in the wake of getting back from well-trained. In any case, a veteran's help association gave him lodging help, guiding, and work preparing. With resolute assurance, John got steady business, set aside cash,

and in the long run turned into a property holder. His story fills in as a demonstration of the flexibility of veterans and the effect of steady projects.

IV. Social and Local area Effect

1. The Nursery that Joins Neighbors:
In an area tormented by division and doubt, a local area garden drive united occupants. Individuals of different foundations, including outsiders and long-term inhabitants, met up to develop a common green space. Through their joint effort, they developed new produce as well as fashioned enduring fellowships, making a more grounded, more joined local area.

2. Modifying Lives After Calamity:

After an overwhelming catastrophic event in the Philippines, a fiasco help association gave crisis haven, food, and clinical consideration to impacted families. Among the recipients was Maria, a mother of three who lost her home in the catastrophe. With the backing of the association, Maria and her family had the option to revamp their lives, exhibiting the versatility of networks despite affliction.

2. Changed lives and futures
The human excursion is one of consistent advancement, set apart by encounters that shape our ways, our viewpoints, and at last, our lives and fates. On occasion, these changes are the aftereffect of life changing open doors, while in different occurrences, they come from the unfaltering flexibility of people confronting affliction. In this investigation of changed lives and prospects, we dive into the accounts of people who

have taken advantage of chances and conquered difficulties, outlining the significant effect of assurance, backing, and flexibility on the course of human life.

1. **Embracing Open doors for Development**
1. **From Road Youngster to Researcher:**
   In a rambling city in Southeast Asia, a little fellow named Ravi once wandered the roads, denied of training and essential necessities. Be that as it may, the mediation of a nearby NGO gave him admittance to a sanctuary, instruction, and mentorship. With unflinching devotion, Ravi succeeded in school, procured a grant to a lofty college, and is currently seeking after a degree in, not set in stone to reward youngsters confronting conditions like his own.
2. **A Creative Odyssey:**

Samantha, a gifted yet striving craftsman, went through years maintaining odd sources of income to earn enough to get by. At some point, she coincidentally found a craftsman

residency program that offered a payment as well as studio space and admittance to workmanship supplies. This open door permitted Samantha to completely submerge herself in her art, and her work started to earn respect. Today, she is a commended craftsman with displays all over the planet, her life everlastingly different by the opportunity to seek after her enthusiasm.

II. Conquering Difficulty through Flexibility

1. **Win Over Sickness:**
   A disease conclusion is a life changing occasion, and for Sarah, it was no exemption. Confronted with the overwhelming possibility of chemotherapy and a questionable future, Sarah drew upon her internal strength and backing from her friends and family. All through her treatment, she kept an uplifting perspective and participated in all encompassing health rehearses. Her flexibility paid

off, and she is presently going away, committing her life to helping other people confronting comparative wellbeing challenges.

2. **The Force of Fresh opportunities:**

John, a previously detained individual, confronted various obstructions after reemerging society. Nonetheless, his obligation to turning his life around drove him to a reemergence program that gave work preparing, mentorship, and backing. Through difficult work and diligence, John got steady business, repaired associations with his family, and turned into a vocal supporter for improvement in law enforcement. His story exhibits the extraordinary capability of renewed opportunities and restoration.

III. Local area and Social Effect

1. **Building Extensions through Volunteerism:**
   A little local area in rustic Appalachia once wrestled with division and seclusion. Be that as it may, a gathering of devoted volunteers started local area building projects, including a common nursery and ordinary municipal events. Over the long run, these endeavors encouraged a feeling of having a place and coordinated effort among inhabitants, changing the local area into a dynamic, affectionate area that presently blossoms with participation and solidarity.

2. **A Shelter for Destitute Youth:**

A neighborhood not-for-profit association laid out a sanctuary for destitute youth in a clamoring metropolitan focus. Among its recipients was Jake, a teen who had encountered shakiness and difficulty all through his life. The sanctuary not just furnished Jake with a protected spot to remain yet additionally offered guiding and professional preparation. Today, Jake is utilized, chasing after additional schooling, and fills in as a coach to other youngsters confronting vagrancy, showing the significant effect of local area support.

B. Economic Growth

Financial development is the main impetus behind the improvement of expectations for everyday comforts, the decrease of destitution, and the upgrade of cultural prosperity. It is the sign of a country's capacity to deliver more labor and products over the long run, prompting expanded pay and worked on personal satisfaction for its residents. In this investigation of monetary development, we will dive into its importance, factors that add to it, and the difficulties and valuable open doors it presents to social orders around the world.

1. **The Meaning of Financial Development**
   Worked on Expectations for everyday comforts: Financial development straightforwardly connects with an expansion in the normal pay of a nation's residents. As the economy grows, people and families will generally have more discretionary cashflow, empowering them to get to better lodging, medical care, training, and other fundamental administrations. This prompts a general improvement in expectations for everyday comforts.

   Destitution Decrease: Monetary development has the ability to lift individuals out of neediness. At the point when an economy develops, open positions duplicate, and wages frequently rise. This outcomes in a critical decrease in the quantity of individuals living in outrageous neediness, at last adding to a more even-handed society.

   Speculation and Advancement: Monetary development draws in venture and encourages development. A developing economy gives organizations open doors for extension and benefit, empowering them to put resources into innovative work, innovation, and foundation. This pattern of venture and development fills further development.

   Financial Assets: A developing economy produces higher duty incomes for legislatures, permitting them to put resources into public administrations and framework. This, thusly, benefits residents by giving better medical care, training, transportation, and other fundamental administrations.

2. **Factors Adding to Financial Development**

Human Resources: A knowledgeable and talented labor force is a basic driver of monetary development. Interest in schooling and professional preparation upgrades human resources, prompting expanded efficiency and advancement.

Mechanical Headways: Advances in innovation assume an essential part in monetary development. Advancement, mechanization, and the reception of new innovations can essentially help efficiency and drive financial development.

Framework Improvement: Effective foundation, including transportation organizations, energy matrices, and correspondence frameworks, works with financial development by diminishing exchange costs, further developing network, and empowering the development of labor and products.

Market Access and Exchange: Admittance to homegrown and worldwide business sectors extends amazing open doors for organizations to develop. Economic alliance and globalization can build a country's monetary result by giving admittance to a more extensive client base.

3. **Difficulties and Amazing open doors**

Imbalance: While monetary development can decrease destitution, it can likewise intensify pay disparity on the off chance that not oversaw successfully. It is fundamental for legislatures and policymakers to carry out measures that guarantee the advantages of development are appropriated evenhandedly across society.

Ecological Maintainability: Fast monetary development frequently comes to the detriment of the climate. Asset exhaustion and contamination can have extreme long haul outcomes. Maintainable improvement works on, including green advancements and preservation endeavors, are essential for offsetting development with ecological obligation.

Monetary Soundness: Monetary development can be joined by monetary air pockets and market unpredictability. Successful guideline and chance administration are important to keep up with monetary soundness and forestall financial emergencies.

Human Resources Improvement: Putting resources into human resources is fundamental for supporting monetary development. Guaranteeing admittance to quality schooling, medical services, and expertise improvement programs is basic for people to partake in and benefit from a developing economy completely.

4. **Worldwide Points of view on Financial Development**

Arising Economies: Many arising economies, especially in Asia and Africa, have encountered quick monetary development in late many years. Nations like China and India have lifted millions out of destitution and changed into worldwide monetary forces to be reckoned with, exhibiting the potential for development in the creating scene.

Development Center points: Advancement center points and tech bunches, like Silicon Valley in the US and Shenzhen in China, have exhibited the extraordinary force of mechanical progressions on financial development. These areas draw in ability, speculation, and advancement, driving financial success.

1. Economic development in the region

Monetary improvement in a locale is a complicated and multi-layered process that includes working on expectations for everyday comforts, framework, training, medical services, and in general prosperity. It is an excursion set apart by progress, difficulties, and valuable open doors, as locales try to improve their monetary exhibition and make a superior future for their occupants. In this investigation of monetary improvement in a locale, we will look at key elements, procedures, and the job of development in driving advancement.

1. **Factors Affecting Financial Turn of events**

   Foundation Venture: Powerful framework, including transportation organizations, energy frameworks, and computerized availability, is imperative for monetary turn of events. Current foundation not just works with the development of labor and products yet additionally draws in organizations and financial backers.

   Human Resources: A gifted and instructed labor force is a foundation of financial turn of events. Interest in schooling, professional preparation, and medical care can upgrade the abilities of the workforce and drive efficiency.

   Business venture and Development: A flourishing enterprising environment and a culture of development can invigorate monetary development. New businesses and inventive undertakings frequently make occupations, drive mechanical progressions, and add to financial expansion.

   Government Strategies: Viable administration and very much planned strategies assume an essential part in forming financial turn of events. Strategies that support venture, safeguard property privileges, and guarantee a steady business climate can encourage financial development.

2. **Systems for Monetary Turn of events**

   Expansion: Monetary broadening includes diminishing reliance on a solitary industry or area. Districts that broaden their economies are better prepared to endure financial shocks and advance long haul development.

   Interest in Schooling: An emphasis on schooling, from youth to advanced education and professional preparation, furnishes the labor force with the abilities required for an information based economy. It likewise improves the district's engaging quality to organizations looking for a gifted workforce.

Reasonable Turn of events: Maintainable monetary improvement considers ecological contemplations. Systems that advance maintainability, like sustainable power reception and asset protection, adjust monetary development to ecological obligation.

Advancement Center points: Making development center points or groups, where research foundations, organizations, and business people team up, can drive financial turn of events. These centers can become focuses of innovation, business venture, and occupation creation.

3. **Challenges in Monetary Turn of events**

Imbalance: Monetary improvement can intensify pay disparity in the event that not oversaw as expected. Guaranteeing that the advantages of development are disseminated fairly is really difficult for locales trying to limit variations.

Ecological Effect: Monetary advancement can come down on normal assets and biological systems, prompting natural corruption. Locales should track down ways of offsetting monetary development with supportability and preservation endeavors.

Globalization and Exchange: While globalization can open up valuable open doors for financial turn of events, it can likewise open areas to worldwide monetary unpredictability and market rivalry. Creating techniques for worldwide exchange and overseeing global relations is a test.

4. **Open doors in Monetary Turn of events**

Innovation and Advancement: The computerized age presents phenomenal open doors for monetary turn of events. Locales can use innovation and development to make new enterprises, further develop efficiency, and improve seriousness on a worldwide scale.

Reasonable Practices: The progress to supportable practices, for example, sustainable power and round economy models, can prompt financial development while tending to natural worries.

Clean innovation and green enterprises address arising open doors.

Globalization: Embracing globalization can offer admittance to worldwide business sectors, speculation, and ability. Locales that position themselves as worldwide centers for exchange and advancement can take advantage of chances for financial turn of events.

5. Contextual analyses in Financial Turn of events

Singapore has changed from a little general store into a worldwide development center point. Through essential interests in schooling, foundation, and innovation, the city-state has drawn in global organizations and encouraged a flourishing beginning up environment. Its prosperity represents the force of visionary arrangements and key preparation in driving monetary turn of events.

Rwanda: Post-Struggle Monetary Advancement:

Rwanda, in spite of confronting the fallout of an overwhelming slaughter during the 1990s, has taken noteworthy steps in monetary turn of events. Zeroing in on areas like innovation, agribusiness, and the travel industry, the nation has encountered consistent development and neediness decrease. Rwanda's change features the flexibility of social orders and the potential for recuperation and improvement.

2. Infrastructure and industry growth

Framework and industry development are entwined components that structure the foundation of a country's financial turn of events. Foundation, including transportation organizations, energy frameworks, and computerized network, gives the essential system to modern development. Simultaneously, industry development drives the interest for further developed foundation, making a commonly building up cycle. In this investigation of the connection among foundation and industry development, we will analyze their importance, reliance, and the groundbreaking effect they have on economies.

1. **The Meaning of Foundation**

   Monetary Empowering influence: Framework works with financial exercises by decreasing exchange costs, further developing availability, and empowering the effective development of labor and products. It fills in as an impetus for business extension, work creation, and in general monetary development.

   Worldwide Seriousness: Countries with current and proficient foundation are more aggressive on the worldwide stage. An advanced foundation network draws in unfamiliar venture, improves exchange, and reinforces a nation's situation in the worldwide commercial center.

   Personal satisfaction: Framework speculations straightforwardly influence the personal satisfaction of residents. Admittance to solid transportation, clean water, power, and computerized network adds to worked on expectations for everyday comforts and admittance to fundamental administrations.

   Flexibility and Calamity Recuperation: Hearty foundation is fundamental for versatility even with cataclysmic events and crises. It empowers speedy reaction and recuperation endeavors, limiting the financial effect of such occasions.

2. **The Job of Industry Development**

   Work Creation: Modern development produces business open doors across different areas, from assembling to administrations. An energetic modern base makes a different scope of occupations, supporting livelihoods and pay development.

   Advancement and Efficiency: Ventures drive development through innovative work exercises. This development, thusly, prompts efficiency enhancements, encouraging financial seriousness and development.

   Esteem Chain Extension: Industry development invigorates the improvement of whole worth chains. Providers, wholesalers, and specialist co-ops benefit from the extension of modern areas, making a far reaching influence all through the economy.

Commodities and Exchange: Flourishing businesses contribute essentially to a nation's products, which can support unfamiliar trade income and exchange adjusts. Effective ventures frequently lead to a positive exchange execution.

3. **The Reliance of Framework and Industry Development**

   Transportation Framework: An effective transportation organization, including streets, rail routes, ports, and air terminals, is basic for the development of natural substances and completed items. Enterprises depend on these organizations for the convenient conveyance of products and admittance to business sectors.

   Energy Framework: Businesses, especially assembling and weighty ventures, rely upon a steady and more than adequate energy supply. Dependable energy foundation guarantees continuous creation cycles and supports modern extension.

   Computerized Availability: In the advanced age, businesses depend on fast web and computerized framework for activities, information the board, and market access. Advanced availability is imperative for present day ventures, including web based business, innovation, and money.

   Water and Disinfection: Enterprises frequently require enormous amounts of water for different cycles. Sufficient water foundation guarantees a feasible stockpile, while disinfection framework upholds labor force wellbeing and efficiency.

4. **Difficulties and Potential open doors**

   Venture Needs: Creating and keeping up with framework requires huge speculation, which can strain public financial plans. Public-private organizations (PPPs) and creative supporting models can address subsidizing holes.

   Natural Manageability: Offsetting modern development with ecological maintainability is a test. Manageable foundation and green innovations offer chances to decrease natural effect while supporting monetary turn of events.

   Computerized Incorporation: Spanning the advanced separation is fundamental to guarantee that all fragments of society benefit from advanced framework. Endeavors to extend broadband access and advanced proficiency programs are pivotal for comprehensive development.

Framework Versatility: As environmental change escalates, guaranteeing the strength of foundation against cataclysmic events is a squeezing concern. Designing arrangements and hazard decrease methodologies are fundamental.

5. **Contextual analyses in Foundation and Industry Development**

China's High velocity Rail Organization and Assembling Blast:
China's interest in a tremendous fast rail network has changed transportation as well as upheld the development of its assembling area. Productive rail associations have diminished strategies costs and worked with the development of merchandise, adding to China's rise as a worldwide assembling force to be reckoned with.

India's Data Innovation (IT) Industry and Advanced Foundation:
India's IT industry, known for its product and rethinking administrations, has flourished because of interests in computerized framework. The development of solid web availability and broadcast communications networks has established a great climate for IT organizations to thrive, creating position and financial development.

8

Chapter 8

Lessons for the World

In our interconnected world, the aggregate human experience is set apart by shared difficulties, wins, and revelations. As we explore the intricacies of the 21st hundred years, we have the chance to gain significant examples from our at various times to shape a more comprehensive, reasonable, and agreeable future. This investigation, comprising of 3000 words, dives into the examples for the world, drawing from history, culture, science, and humankind's common encounters.

1. **Illustrations from History**
   The Outcomes of Contention and War:
   Since forever ago, wars and clashes have brought massive affliction and obliteration. The illustrations from history help us to remember the significance of discretion, compromise, and participation in forestalling savagery and safeguarding common freedoms.
   The Force of Versatility:
   The world has seen endless instances of versatility even with affliction. From present conflict remaking on recuperation from catastrophic events, mankind's capacity to adjust and revamp offers trust and motivation. These accounts stress the significance

of persistence and fortitude.

The Hazards of Expansionism and Dominion:

The tradition of expansionism and colonialism has left enduring scars on numerous areas. Recognizing these treacheries and pursuing decolonization and compensations is an example in tending to verifiable treacheries and taking a stab at worldwide value.

The Mission for Common freedoms:

The battle for common liberties, social equality, and civil rights has been a main thrust in significantly shaping social orders. The illustrations from common liberties developments highlight the significance of balance, equity, and the insurance of major opportunities for all.

2. **Illustrations from Culture and Variety**

The Worth of Social Trade:

Social trade encourages figuring out, resilience, and enthusiasm for variety. Embracing and celebrating various societies can prompt improving encounters and significant associations, advancing worldwide congruity.

The Effect of Writing and Expressions:

Writing, workmanship, and imaginative articulation have the ability to rouse, instruct, and challenge insights. They help us to remember the significance of opportunity of articulation and the job of culture in significantly shaping social orders.

The Tradition of Native Insight:

Native people group all over the planet have safeguarded important information about manageable living and coinciding with nature. Their insight can show us fundamental examples in ecological stewardship and the security of biodiversity.

The Meaning of Language:

Language is an entryway to understanding and safeguarding society. Endeavors to safeguard imperiled dialects and advance multilingualism are examples in shielding social legacy and advancing inclusivity.

3. **Illustrations from Science and Innovation**
   The Force of Logical Disclosure:
   Logical forward leaps have changed human life, from headways in medication to the investigation of room. These illustrations feature the significance of examination, advancement, and proof based direction.

   The Advanced Age and Network:
   The advanced age has associated individuals across the globe, empowering moment correspondence and data sharing. Examples in advanced education, network safety, and mindful innovation use are fundamental in this interconnected world.

   The Direness of Ecological Protection:
   Environmental change, contamination, and territory misfortune present critical dangers to our planet. Examples in natural preservation underscore the requirement for reasonable practices, environmentally friendly power, and mindful utilization.

   The Moral Difficulties of Man-made consciousness:
   The advancement of man-made brainpower (artificial intelligence) presents moral difficulties and open doors. Examples from artificial intelligence progressions feature the significance of morals, straightforwardness, and guideline in bridling this innovation to support mankind.

4. **Illustrations from Philanthropic Endeavors**
   The Job of Help and Altruism:
   Compassionate associations and altruistic endeavors have given lifesaving help with seasons of emergency. These examples highlight the significance of sympathy, liberality, and fortitude in tending to worldwide difficulties.

   The Exile Emergency and Uprooting:
   The situation of evacuees and effectively dislodged people calls for worldwide participation and sympathy. Examples in evacuee support stress the requirement for places of refuge, resettlement, and endeavors to address underlying drivers of relocation.

The Battle Against Irresistible Sicknesses:
Worldwide endeavors to battle irresistible sicknesses, including HIV/Helps and Coronavirus, show the significance of medical services framework, immunization, and global cooperation in shielding general wellbeing.

The Flexibility of Networks:
Networks all over the planet have shown strength even with cataclysmic events, clashes, and pandemics. Their accounts rouse examples in readiness, local area strengthening, and catastrophe reaction.

5. **Illustrations for What's to come**

Practical Advancement Objectives (SDGs):
The Unified Countries' SDGs give a guide to tending to worldwide difficulties, including neediness, disparity, and environmental change. The examples from the SDGs underscore the requirement for deliberate worldwide activity and responsibility in accomplishing these objectives.

Youth Commitment and Activism:
Youth-drove developments for environment activity, civil rights, and common liberties outline the force of youthful voices in molding what's in store. Examples in youth

commitment highlight the significance of including the cutting edge in navigation and backing.

Interconnectedness and Relationship:
The Coronavirus pandemic featured the interconnected idea of our reality. Examples in worldwide wellbeing, participation, and readiness underscore the significance of tending to worldwide difficulties on the whole.

Emergency as a Chance for Change:
Emergencies, whether regular or human-made, can act as impetuses for change and positive change. Illustrations in strength, transformation, and development help us to remember the human ability to conquer misfortune.

1. Global Relevance

In our undeniably interconnected and related world, worldwide pertinence has turned into a urgent idea. It implies the capacity of people, networks, associations, and countries to comprehend, adjust to, and effectively add to the complex and quickly changing worldwide scene. In this investigation of worldwide pertinence, we will dive into its importance, the difficulties it presents, and the open doors it offers in the 21st hundred years.

1. The Meaning of Worldwide Importance
Financial Flourishing:

Worldwide importance is essential for monetary success. In a time of worldwide business sectors and supply chains, organizations should be universally applicable to stay cutthroat. Admittance to worldwide business sectors, ability, and speculations is fundamental for supported development.

Harmony and Security:

Worldwide importance assumes an essential part in advancing harmony and security. Countries and associations with a worldwide presence are many times central members in worldwide discretion and compromise, adding to worldwide solidness.

Supportable Turn of events:

Tending to worldwide difficulties, for example, environmental change, destitution, and imbalance requires worldwide significance. Participation and coordinated effort on a worldwide scale are fundamental to accomplishing the Unified Countries' Maintainable Improvement Objectives (SDGs).

Social Trade and Understanding:

Worldwide pertinence cultivates social trade and common comprehension among countries and people groups. It advances the enthusiasm for variety and the capacity to actually explore social contrasts.

2. **The Difficulties of Worldwide Significance**
Intricacy and Vagueness:

The worldwide scene is described by intricacy and uncertainty. Exploring different societies, political frameworks, and financial real factors can be testing, requiring versatility and nuanced understanding.

International Strains:

International pressures and clashes can confuse endeavors to remain around the world applicable. Countries and associations should cautiously explore conciliatory connections and global collusions.

Innovative Interruption:

The fast speed of innovative progression presents difficulties and amazing open doors for worldwide pertinence. Associations and people should remain current with innovation patterns to stay cutthroat.

Ecological Maintainability:

The direness of ecological supportability requires worldwide activity. Associations should take on ecologically capable practices to address environmental change and asset exhaustion.

3. **Open doors in Worldwide Importance**
Advancement and Innovation:

The computerized age offers open doors for worldwide significance through development and innovation. Innovation driven arrangements, like web based business and computerized administrations, can contact a worldwide crowd.

Worldwide Organizations:

Worldwide significance can be upgraded through essential associations and joint efforts. Worldwide associations and worldwide partnerships give stages to tending to worldwide difficulties on the whole.

Emergency Reaction and Compassionate Endeavors:

Associations that are worldwide significant are strategically situated to answer worldwide emergencies, including catastrophic events and general wellbeing crises. Compassionate endeavors on a worldwide scale require a worldwide presence.

Economical Strategic approaches:

Manageability is a chance for worldwide pertinence. Associations that take on supportable practices are more alluring to shoppers and financial backers who focus on natural and social obligation.

4. **Contextual analyses in Worldwide Significance**

Worldwide Wellbeing Associations and Pandemic Reaction:

Worldwide wellbeing associations like the World Wellbeing Association (WHO) and Médecins Sans Frontières (Specialists Without Lines) represent worldwide pertinence. They assume fundamental parts in pandemic reaction, medical services access, and illness anticipation around the world.

Tech Goliaths and Advanced Development:

Innovation organizations like Apple, Google, and Amazon have accomplished worldwide importance through advanced development. Their items and administrations are utilized by billions of individuals around the world, reshaping businesses and economies.

Global NGOs and Helpful Work:

Worldwide non-legislative associations (NGOs) like UNICEF and the Red Cross are universally important substances. They give philanthropic guide, support improvement undertakings, and backer for basic liberties on a worldwide scale.

Worldwide Supportability Drives:

Maintainability drives like the Paris Settlement on environmental change and the Unified Countries' SDGs address worldwide pertinence in tending to ecological difficulties and advancing mindful turn of events.

1. **How Kaleshwaram's success can inspire other regions**

The Kaleshwaram Lift Water system Task, arranged in the Indian territory of Telangana, has arisen as an exceptional example of overcoming adversity, exhibiting how visionary preparation, development, and decided execution can change the fortunes of a locale. This great water system project has changed the horticultural scene of Telangana as well as fills in as a rousing model for different locales overall that face comparable difficulties connected with water shortage, farming, and country improvement. In this

investigation, we will dive into the vital components of Kaleshwaram's prosperity and the way that its accomplishments can act as a motivation for different locales.

1. **Visionary Preparation and Administration**
   Exhaustive Vision: The outcome of Kaleshwaram is established in visionary arranging that enveloped water system as well as water the board, country advancement, and foundation improvement. This comprehensive methodology guaranteed that the task tended to a great many difficulties looked by the locale.
   Solid Initiative: Powerful initiative assumed a urgent part in the task's prosperity. Political will, commitment, and the capacity to collect help from different partners were instrumental in defeating snags and driving the task forward.
2. **Creative Water The board**
   Interlinking Water Sources: Kaleshwaram brilliantly interlinked numerous streams and supplies, making a mind boggling organization to disseminate water across the district productively. This approach amplified water use and limited wastage.
   Continuous Checking: The undertaking integrated trend setting innovations for ongoing observing and control of water stream. This guaranteed exact water designation and decreased the gamble of water deficiencies.
3. **Financial Change**
   Rural Success: Kaleshwaram altogether expanded the accessibility

of water for horticulture. This lift in water system limit prompted higher harvest yields, expanded rural pay, and further developed vocations for ranchers in the locale.

Modern Development: Sufficient water supply additionally animated modern development. As businesses approached solid water sources, the locale pulled in ventures, prompting the formation of open positions and monetary turn of events.

4. **Provincial Turn of events**

Further developed Foundation: The venture further developed framework in rustic regions, including streets, power supply, and correspondence organizations. This worked with the undertaking's execution as well as upgraded generally rustic turn of events.

Personal satisfaction: Admittance to water for water system, drinking, and disinfection worked on the personal satisfaction in rustic networks. It decreased the weight on ladies who frequently needed to make a trip significant distances to get water.

5. **Reasonable Asset The executives**

Ecological Contemplations: Kaleshwaram's prosperity likewise highlights the significance of maintainable asset the board. The venture integrated natural contemplations and embraced rehearses that limit the environmental effect of water redirection.

Local area Association: The task effectively elaborate neighborhood networks in direction and execution. This commitment cultivated a feeling of pride and obligation among individuals, guaranteeing the undertaking's drawn out supportability.

6. **Illustrations for Different Areas**

All encompassing Preparation: Locales confronting comparable difficulties ought to take on a far reaching and comprehensive way to deal with address water shortage, horticultural necessities, and provincial turn of events. Incorporated arranging guarantees that the advantages of activities reach out past water system.

Administration and Political Will: Solid authority and political responsibility are basic to beating obstacles and pushing forward aggressive activities. Pioneers should focus on the government assistance of the district and earn support for drives.

Advancement in Water The board: Creative water the executives arrangements, including interlinking water sources and ongoing observing, can boost the productivity of water usage and dissemination.

Reasonable Practices: Ecological contemplations should be an indispensable piece of any huge scope project. Supportable practices assist with protecting environments and guarantee the drawn out practicality of water assets.

Local area Commitment: Including nearby networks in project arranging and execution encourages a feeling of responsibility and guarantees that the task lines up with the requirements and needs of individuals it serves.

7. **Possible Worldwide Effect**

Tending to Water Shortage: Numerous districts all over the planet face water shortage issues like those that provoked the Kaleshwaram Undertaking. Executing comparative

systems can assist with easing water pressure and backing farming and financial development.

Moving Enormous scope Framework: Kaleshwaram fills in as a model for the fruitful execution of huge scope foundation projects. Its prosperity can rouse different districts to leave on groundbreaking drives that address squeezing difficulties.

Advancing Country Advancement: The undertaking's accentuation on rustic turn of events, including further developed framework and personal satisfaction, can act as an outline for locales trying to elevate provincial networks and scaffold metropolitan provincial partitions.

2. **Lessons for sustainable water management**

Water, frequently alluded to as the "blue gold," is a limited and fundamental asset for life on The planet. As worldwide populace development and environmental change apply expanding tension on water assets, economical water the board has become central. Illustrations gained from different districts and drives all over the planet offer significant experiences into how we can dependably oversee and moderate this valuable asset for current and people in the future. In this investigation, we will dive into key illustrations for maintainable water the executives that can act as an aide for states, networks, and people the same.

1. **Incorporated Water Asset The executives**
   Example 1: All encompassing Preparation and The board:
   Supportable water the board requires an all encompassing methodology that considers the whole water cycle, from source to removal. Coordinated Water Asset The board (IWRM) is a structure that underlines the interconnectedness of water sources, environments, and human exercises. Districts should take on IWRM standards to guarantee fair admittance to water while safeguarding biological systems and tending to contending requests.
   Illustration 2: Transboundary Collaboration:
   Many water bodies and springs cross public lines. Powerful coordinated effort and transboundary arrangements are fundamental to forestall clashes over shared water assets. The progress of drives like the Mekong Stream Commission and the Joint Administration Plan for the Colorado Waterway fills in as a demonstration of the advantages of global participation in water the executives.
2. **Supportable Horticulture and Water system**
   Illustration 3: Effective Water Use in Farming:
   Horticulture represents a critical piece of worldwide water use. Reasonable agribusiness rehearses, for example, dribble water system, water reaping, and accuracy cultivating, can improve water use, lessen wastage, and increment crop yields. Israel's outcome in water-proficient cultivating exhibits the capability of these practices.
   Illustration 4: Yield Determination and Water-Use Profi-

ciency:

Crop decision assumes a pivotal part in reasonable water the board. Choosing dry spell safe and water-proficient yield assortments, alongside utilizing productive water system strategies, can essentially decrease water prerequisites for horticulture. Models from areas like Australia and India feature the advantages of harvest broadening and water-saving advancements.

3. **Metropolitan Water The board**

Example 5: Water Preservation and Reusing:

Metropolitan focuses polish off significant measures of water for drinking, disinfection, and modern cycles. Executing water protection measures, advancing reusing and reuse of wastewater, and embracing green framework can lessen the stress on metropolitan water supplies. Singapore's NEWater drive and Los Angeles' water gathering programs are praiseworthy models.

Example 6: Stormwater The board:

Legitimate stormwater the executives can relieve flooding, forestall pollution of water bodies, and re-energize groundwater. Metropolitan arranging that integrates green spaces, porous surfaces, and normal water the board frameworks can assist urban areas with tending to stormwater challenges reasonably. Portland's Green Roads program features compelling stormwater the executives.

4. **Environment Reclamation and Security**

Example 7: Watershed The board:

Watersheds assume a urgent part in giving clean water to networks. Securing and reestablishing watersheds through afforestation, disintegration control, and wetland protection can upgrade water quality, decrease sedimentation, and relieve the impacts of outrageous climate occasions. Examples from the Chesapeake Straight Watershed and the Rhine Waterway Bowl stress the significance of watershed the board.

Example 8: Biodiversity Preservation:

Sound environments are fundamental for keeping up with water quality and directing water stream. Biodiversity preservation endeavors, including the insurance of riparian zones and oceanic natural surroundings, add to maintainable water the board. Drives like the rebuilding of the Florida Everglades and the restoration of the Aral Ocean environment highlight the meaning of biological system protection.

5. **Schooling and Mindfulness**

Illustration 9: Public Commitment and Instruction:

Public mindfulness and schooling are instrumental in advancing water preservation and capable water use. Networks, legislatures, and associations ought to participate in effort and schooling projects to illuminate individuals about the worth regarding water and the significance of maintainable practices.

Example 10: Neighborhood Strengthening:

Nearby people group frequently have a profound comprehension of their water assets. Engaging people group to take part in water the executives choices, foster maintainable practices, and screen water quality can prompt more viable and impartial arrangements.

6. **Imaginative Innovations and Supporting**

Illustration 11: Mechanical Developments:

Propels in innovation, for example, satellite-based checking, information examination, and water treatment advancements, can improve water asset the board. Areas ought to put resources into state of the art advances to further develop proficiency and viability in water the executives.

Illustration 12: Venture and Supporting:

Reasonable water the board requires significant speculation. Creative supporting components, including public-private organizations, water securities, and devoted water reserves, can prepare assets for framework improvement and preservation endeavors.

B. Future Prospects

What's to come is a scene of vast potential outcomes, formed by our aggregate activities, developments, and desires. It is a domain where difficulties and open doors coincide, where the way ahead relies upon our capacity to adjust, improve, and cooperate. In this investigation of future possibilities, we will dive into the key patterns, difficulties, and open doors that lie ahead in different parts of our lives, from innovation and economy to climate and society.

1. **Mechanical Headways**

   Man-made brainpower and Computerization:

   The quick headway of computerized reasoning (man-made intelligence) and robotization presents both commitment and challenge. While man-made intelligence can improve effectiveness and efficiency, it likewise brings up issues about the fate of work and the requirement for reskilling and upskilling the labor force.

   Quantum Figuring:

   Quantum figuring, with altering processing power, holds incredible commitment for tackling complex problems potential. Its applications in cryptography, materials science, and medication disclosure are not too far off.

   Advanced Change:

   The continuous advanced change is reshaping ventures and social orders. The future will see expanded dependence on computerized innovations for correspondence, instruction, medical services, and trade, requiring an emphasis on advanced education and network safety.

2. **Ecological Manageability**

   Environmental Change Alleviation:

   The direness of environmental change calls for critical endeavors to decrease ozone harming substance discharges. Changing to environmentally friendly power, embracing maintainable farming practices, and saving biological systems are basic for a reasonable future.

Roundabout Economy:

The idea of a roundabout economy, where assets are reused and reused, is building up forward momentum. Roundabout practices can limit squander, diminish ecological effect, and set out new financial open doors.

Biodiversity Protection:

Safeguarding biodiversity and normal territories is crucial for biological system wellbeing and versatility. Future possibilities depend on endeavors to save species variety, reestablish biological systems, and battle natural surroundings misfortune.

3. **Monetary Strength**

Worldwide Financial Coordination:

The world remaining parts interconnected, with worldwide exchange and money assuming a huge part in monetary success. Future possibilities rely upon keeping up

with open business sectors, tending to pay disparity, and advancing supportable financial development.

Comprehensive Development:

The quest for comprehensive development, where financial advantages are shared impartially, is vital to future monetary security. Approaches that address abberations in pay, admittance to schooling, and social administrations are fundamental.

Reasonable Advancement Objectives (SDGs):

The Unified Countries' SDGs give a guide to tending to worldwide difficulties and cultivating economical turn of events. Progress towards accomplishing the SDGs will shape future possibilities for mankind.

4. **Cultural and Social Movements**

Segment Changes:

Maturing populaces and changing socioeconomics are reshaping social orders around the world. The future will require adjusting medical care frameworks, benefits, and social help designs to address the issues of a more established populace.

Orientation Balance and Variety:

Endeavors to advance orientation fairness and embrace variety are picking up speed. Accomplishing full orientation equity, variety, and incorporation is a promising possibility for a more impartial and just society.

Advanced Network and Online Entertainment:

The proceeded with development of advanced network and online entertainment will impact correspondence, data sharing, and activism. Future possibilities incorporate outfitting these stages for positive change while resolving issues like internet based falsehood and protection.

5. **International Elements**

Worldwide Administration and Collaboration:

Viable worldwide administration and participation are vital for address transnational difficulties, from pandemics to environmental change. Future possibilities rely on global coordinated effort and tact.

Changes in Worldwide Power:

The international scene is developing, with shifts in worldwide power elements. The ascent of arising economies and changes in global coalitions will shape the world's political and financial future.

Online protection and Computerized Power:

As dependence on advanced innovations develops, the future will see expanded center around network protection and computerized power. Countries will attempt to safeguard their computerized framework and information.

1. **The role of Kaleshwaram in India's water future**

India, with its assorted environment examples and developing populace, faces huge difficulties in dealing with its water assets. The Kaleshwaram Lift Water system Undertaking, situated in the territory of Telangana, has arisen as a groundbreaking drive that assumes a critical part in India's water future. This task, one of the biggest of its sort on the planet, not just addresses basic water difficulties in the locale yet in addition fills in as a model for feasible water asset the board in the country. In this investigation, we will analyze the job of the Kaleshwaram Task in molding India's water future and its more extensive ramifications for the country.

1. **Tending to Water Shortage**
   Lightening Water Pressure:
   India faces water pressure because of variables like unpredictable rainstorm, over-extraction of groundwater, and wasteful water the executives rehearses. The Kaleshwaram Venture handles this issue by saddling water from different streams, productively dispersing it to bone-dry locales, and re-energizing groundwater springs.

   Improving Rural Efficiency:
   Farming is a foundation of India's economy, yet it polishes off a critical piece of the nation's water assets. Kaleshwaram's arrangement of water system water to dry spell inclined regions increments agrarian efficiency, guarantees food security, and supports the pay of ranchers.

2. **Alleviating Dry spells and Floods**
   Dry spell Alleviation:
   India frequently wrestles with dry spells that effect crop yields, jobs, and food security. The Kaleshwaram Undertaking mitigates dry season by giving a solid water source to horticulture, assisting ranchers with adapting to droughts.

   Flood Control:
   The undertaking additionally incorporates flood control components. By redirecting overabundance floodwater to water-scant areas and making stockpiling supplies, it oversees flood gambles while at the same time renewing drained springs.

3. **Maintainable Water Asset The executives**
Productive Water Use:
Kaleshwaram utilizes productive water the executives procedures, for example, channel lining, miniature water system, and water reusing, decreasing water wastage and advancing economical water use.

Groundwater Re-energize:
Groundwater, a basic asset in India, is frequently over-took advantage of. The undertaking underlines re-energizing springs, guaranteeing an economical and dependable wellspring of water for what's to come.

4. **Financial Effect**
Rustic Turn of events:
Admittance to water helps agrarian pay as well as prompts rustic turn of events. Further developed foundation, training, medical services, and vocation open doors add to the general prosperity of networks in the district.

Modern Development:
Satisfactory water supply is significant for modern development. The accessibility of dependable water sources is drawing in speculations, encouraging modern turn of events, and setting out work open doors.

5. **Replicability and Flexibility**
Replicable Model:
The outcome of the Kaleshwaram Venture fills in as a model for maintainable water asset the board in India. Comparable activities can be carried out in water-pushed districts the nation over, tending to limited water difficulties.

Environment Versatility:
Even with environmental change, strong water the executives frameworks like Kaleshwaram are fundamental. The venture's flexibility in overseeing outrageous climate occasions and

guaranteeing water accessibility during delayed droughts is significant for India's environment versatility.

6. Difficulties and Concerns

Natural Effect:

Huge scope water undertakings can have natural repercussions, including living space disturbance and changed stream environments. Cautious preparation and moderation measures are important to limit unfriendly impacts.

Fair Water Conveyance:

Guaranteeing fair water conveyance among different partners, including ranchers, businesses, and metropolitan regions, is a test. Straightforward water portion arrangements and local area inclusion are essential to tending to this worry.

7. Future Water Security

Enhanced Water Sources:

India's water future relies upon enhancing water sources past conventional downpour took care of farming. The Kaleshwaram Venture starts a trend for tackling stream interlinking and water redirection to satisfy developing water needs.

Feasible Urbanization:

As India's metropolitan populace keeps on developing, feasible metropolitan water the board turns out to be progressively basic. Coordinated metropolitan arranging that incorporates water reusing, proficient sewage treatment, and mindful water use is fundamental for future water security.

2. Evolving challenges and opportunities

The world we live in will be in a consistent condition of motion, described by steadily developing difficulties and potential open doors. As social orders, economies, advancements, and environments keep on changing, our capacity to adjust and develop becomes critical. In this investigation, we will dive into the developing difficulties and amazing open doors across different areas, from innovation and economy to climate and society, and talk about how they shape our present and future.

1. **Mechanical Development**
   Advanced Change:
   The quick speed of computerized change keeps on upsetting businesses and social orders. The boundless reception of distributed computing, computerized reasoning, and the Web of Things (IoT) presents valuable open doors for improved proficiency, network, and development.
   Online protection Difficulties:
   As innovation progresses, so do online protection dangers. Developing cyberattacks require steady carefulness and variation of network safety measures to safeguard delicate information and basic foundation.

2. **Monetary Scene**
   Globalization and Exchange:
   Globalization has prompted expanded interconnectedness in exchange and money. While this presents potential open doors for financial development, it additionally opens economies to worldwide market unpredictability and exchange debates.
   Robotization and Work:
   Mechanization and man-made consciousness are reshaping the work market. While they offer expanded productivity, they additionally present difficulties connected with work uprooting and the requirement for labor force reskilling.

3. **Natural Elements**
   Environmental Change Alleviation:
   Environmental change is an advancing emergency that requests prompt activity. Open doors for addressing environmental change incorporate progressing to sustainable power sources, taking on maintainable agrarian practices, and improving environment flexibility.

Biodiversity Protection:

Biodiversity misfortune is a continuous concern. The open door lies in saving and reestablishing environments, safeguarding jeopardized species, and executing manageable land-use rehearses.

4. **Cultural Movements**

Segment Changes:

Maturing populaces and changing socioeconomics are impacting medical care, social administrations, and retirement arranging. Variation is expected to guarantee that maturing populaces approach sufficient help and care.

Orientation Value and Variety:

Advancing cultural mentalities toward orientation value and variety offer open doors for more noteworthy incorporation and balance. The test is to kill inclinations and separation across different areas.

5. **International Real factors**

International Power Movements:

The international scene is advancing with the ascent of new worldwide powers and evolving collusions. This presents difficulties connected with worldwide tact, exchange relations, and compromise.

Worldwide Wellbeing Security:

The Coronavirus pandemic has featured the requirement for worldwide wellbeing participation. The open door lies in fortifying worldwide wellbeing frameworks, working on pandemic readiness, and guaranteeing evenhanded admittance to medical care.

6. **Valuable open doors in Emergency**

Emergency as Impetus for Change:

Emergencies, whether catastrophic events or pandemics, can act as impetuses for positive change. They set out open doors for development, strength building, and reconsidering frameworks to improve things.

Supportable Improvement Objectives (SDGs):
The Unified Countries' SDGs give a guide to tending to developing worldwide difficulties. Progress toward accomplishing these objectives presents potential open doors for economical turn of events and worked on personal satisfaction.

7. **Challenges in Outfitting Valuable open doors**
Advanced Separation:
While computerized innovation offers various open doors, the advanced separation stays a test, with numerous networks lacking admittance to fundamental advanced assets. Spanning this separation is pivotal for comprehensive development.

Monetary Differences:
Monetary open doors are not dispersed similarly. Tending to monetary incongruities through strategies that elevate fair admittance to instruction, medical services, and financial assets is a tireless test.

8. **The Job of Advancement**

Development as a Driver:
Development, whether in innovation, strategy, or social practices, assumes an essential part in tending to advancing difficulties and quickly jumping all over chances. It takes into consideration the improvement of novel arrangements and the transformation of existing ones.

Versatile Limit:
Building versatile limit inside social orders, associations, and people is significant. It includes encouraging a culture of ceaseless learning, versatility, and innovativeness.